ALSO BY M[

The Fate of America: An [

"Our nation leads the worl[   ]ver-increasing
technological capacity and excellence. Why is it we are not
equally dominant in the race for spiritual excellence? This
fascinating, insightful, psychological profile of the American
psyche offers answers that both enlighten and stimulate."

— MARIO CUOMO

"A large-scale analysis of this country on a par with
Tocqueville . . . an important book. It raises serious questions
about our country, makes perceptive observations about our
culture, and provokes us to look inside ourselves in a
critical, yet constructive, way."

— HOWARD ZINN,
author of *A People's History of the United States*

"A broad-ranging, cogently argued, and provocative
critique that has taken on a whole new dimension
since September 11."

— LIBRARY JOURNAL

Modern Mysticism: Jung, Zen and the Still Good Hand of God

"A psychotherapist writes that rarest of works—a look at the wondrous and mysterious worlds of the unconscious mind, moving from the paranormal to the highest spiritual experience."

– SOPHY BURNHAM,
author of *A Book of Angels*

"Gellert takes you with him, into the whale's belly and out! An extraordinary experience—not to be wished for and not to be missed!"

– DIANE WOLKSTEIN,
author of *The First Love Stories*

"This book is wonderful, as it is both challenging and comforting. I highly recommend it to anyone who is serious about spirituality."

– RABBI ARTHUR GROSS-SCHAEFER

THE WAY OF THE SMALL

A Jung on the Hudson Book Series Selection

The Jung on the Hudson Book Series was instituted by the New York Center for Jungian Studies in 1997. This ongoing series is designed to present books that will be of interest to individuals of all fields, including mental health professionals, who are interested in exploring the relevance of the psychology and ideas of C. G. Jung to their personal lives and professional activities.

For more information about this series, the annual Jung on the Hudson seminars, and the New York Center for Jungian Studies contact: Aryeh Maidenbaum, Ph.D., New York Center for Jungian Studies, 27. N. Chestnut St., Ste. 3, New Paltz, NY 12561-1708, telephone (845) 256-0191, fax (845) 256-0196.

For more information about becoming part of this series contact: Yvonne Paglia, Nicolas-Hays, P. O. Box 540206, Lake Worth, FL 33454-0206, email: info@nicolashays.com.

THE WAY
OF THE
SMALL

why less
is truly more

Michael Gellert

WITH A FOREWORD BY **THOMAS MOORE**

NICOLAS-HAYS, INC.
Lake Worth, Florida

First published in 2008 by
Nicolas-Hays, Inc.
P. O. Box 540206 • Lake Worth, FL 33454-0206
www.nicolashays.com
Distributed to the trade by Red Wheel/Weiser, LLC
65 Parker St., Unit 7 • Newburyport, MA 01950-4600
www.redwheelweiser.com

Library of Congress Cataloging-in-Publication data
Gellert, Michael.
The way of the small : why less is truly more / Michael Gellert ; with a foreword by Thomas Moore.
p. cm.
Includes bibliographical references and index.
ISBN-13: 978-0-89254-129-4 (alk. paper)
ISBN-10: 0-89254-129-6 (alk. paper)
1. Simplicity (Philosophy) 2. Simplicity--Religious aspects. 3. Spirituality.
4. Self-esteem. 5. Conduct of life. I. Title.
B105.S55G45 2008
204'.4--dc22   2007035671
VG
Cover and text design by Kathryn Sky-Peck

Printed in the United States of America
12 11 10 09 08 07 06
7 6 5 4 3 2 1

Grateful acknowledgment is made for permission to reproduce the following material: "How happy is the little stone," by Emily Dickinson. Reprinted by permission of the publishers and the Trustees of Amherst College from *The Poems of Emily Dickinson*, Thomas H. Johnson, ed., Cambridge, Mass.: The Belknap Press of Harvard University Press, Copyright © 1951, 1955, 1979, 1983 by the President and Fellows of Harvard College. Submitted excerpt from "The Man Watching" [23 II] from *Selected Poems of Rainer Maria Rilke, A Translation from the German and Commentary by Robert Bly*. Copyright © 1981 by Robert Bly. Reprinted by permission of HarperCollins Publishers. "The Guest House," by Jelaluddin Balkhi Rumi. From *The Illuminated Rumi* by Coleman Barks and Michael Green, copyright © 1997 by Coleman Barks and Michael Green. Used by permission of Broadway Books, a division of Random House, Inc. Reprinted also by permission of Reid Boates Literary Agency. The chapter entitled "God's Small Secret," copyright by Michael Gellert, was published in an earlier form in *Psychological Perspectives*, Vol. 48, Issue 1, 2005, Routledge: Taylor & Francis Group, Philadelphia, PA.

For Gilda, Betty, and Gary,
wayfarers of the small

❧

*Many years of work on these matters have completely convinced me
not only that small is beautiful but also that small
is possible and has the future on its side.*

[E.F. SCHUMACHER]

*If you fail to seek God in the small things,
you will seek him in vain for the large things.*

[ANDREW MURRAY]

CONTENTS

PART ONE:

WHAT IS THE WAY OF THE SMALL?

PART TWO:

ESSENTIAL PRINCIPLES FOR LIVING SMALL

7. Practicing the Way of the Small in the World 135

*A Slice of Smallness • Humility is the Highest Form of
Greatness • Approaching Diversity and Complexity by Way of the
Small • The World Scorns the Small • Dealing With Your Own
Shadow • Learning to Listen to Silence • Potent Quotes*

FOREWORD

by Thomas Moore

I love Mondays. No traveling across the world. No parties and gatherings and events. Nothing but an ordinary day's work, at home, in my precious tiny room.

The life of the writer is odd in that he sits at his desk many hours a day and once in a while discovers that his words have gone out into the far distant world. I enjoy this way of life. I can spend my days at home and yet make a little contribution to the greater community.

In all my books I praise the small and the ordinary. I have a natural antipathy toward "spiritual" writings that are inflated—too big in scope, too focused on universals and ultimates. For years I've been criticized for not speaking of moral absolutes. I have enough trouble sorting out everyday ethical decisions.

I like to write forewords and small essays, even blurbs. I see them as miniatures. A tiny painting or jewel is worth at least as much as a grand wall-sized canvas or a major cathedral or temple.

For years now I have taught at Schumacher College in Devon, England, named for the author of *Small is Beautiful.*

There, I learn spiritual simplicity from my wise spiritual advisor and friend, Satish Kumar. He founded The Small School and the college, which has a limit of twenty-five students per course. He has revealed to me the power of small acts and limited ambitions.

Now I have further wisdom and support from Michael Gellert in this inspired little book about the small and the simple. What I like most about it is the paradox that lies between the words and the covers: learn to live small and you will discover great pleasures. You will accomplish more in your life than you could ever predict if you were overly ambitious.

It does no good to romanticize the small. Once, I was asked to speak at a conference on the small, and, with my usual contrariness, I gave a lecture on the big and huge. I wanted to keep the small from becoming too big. You can overdo something that is almost negligible in size. Sometimes, as soon as you start to rhapsodize on the small, it gets too big.

But this book avoids the trap of inflating the small. It explores many facets of the simple life. Amazingly, it doesn't literalize or romanticize. It is steady and wise and grounded. I feel at home in it. I especially appreciate the dream told at the end, of a small cabin that inside contains a big world. It's like a person. We look small in relation to the horizon, but we are a microcosm, an intricate cosmos of thoughts and passions. The ancient philosophers said that we have a whole world inside of us, including a sun and moon and planets.

As long as we live small, those interior planets spin and hum. They give our simple acts their enormous power. They give our words cosmic resonance. They make of our local lives the magnetic power to hold together our communities, our cultures, and our planet.

This is a jewel of a book. There is a pearl inside it. Read the words closely, and you will discover that pearl—elusive, precious, and tiny.

INTRODUCTION

Remember: very little is needed to make a happy life.

[MARCUS AURELIUS]

This book is a journey into the small. It draws upon the age-old teaching that simplicity is the key to a good life. When we live small, we live with limits and according to our means, in a way that is not inflated either economically or psychologically. This helps us to find success and happiness not only materially, but spiritually. It also helps us cope with such diminishing ordeals as failure, illness, the loss of a loved one, and aging. Living small raises the monotony of daily life to a godly level and reveals God in the little and difficult things. It makes everyday life sacred.

Although I was familiar with this simple and ancient way of living from my work as a Jungian analyst and my training in Judaism, religious studies, and Zen, it wasn't until a personally trying period of darkness that I truly discovered its dynamic principles. Brain surgery, a divorce, some other heartbreaking disappointments, and 9/11—all occurring close together—had left me with haunting feelings of vulnerability, failure, and emptiness. Each successive event further convinced me how small and insignificant my life was, and I fell into a depression.

After two years in this state of diminishment, I came to the conclusion that the only honest way to deal with it was to squarely face its victory over me. "*This is it,*" I said to myself, "*this is my life.*" Accepting this defeat was difficult, and for some time my sadness was coupled with brooding. Eventually, however, it became clear to me that the *diminishment itself* was what was significant here. There was something very sobering and freeing about seeing how small I was. The pressure to be anything other than what I was had been lifted. By embracing the smallness of my life, the situation gradually shifted from being a problem to being a deeper way of living, even if that way was constricted. This did not magically transform my hardships, but altered my view of them. Instead of being unwanted intrusions in my life, they became a source of mystery and meaning—that is, sacred.

Finally one day, with these hardships no more resolved or under control than before, I recognized an old, familiar feeling but in a new form: I was happy. What was new was that it was unattached to any particular event, person, or situation. Paradoxically, I was able to experience a sense of well-being even though I was suffering. This was how I came to understand the relationship between the way of the small and happiness. True happiness is an acceptance of life *as it is given to us*, with its diminishment, mystery, uncontrollability, and all. Darkness, too, is a part of everyday life, and the suffering it brings needs to also be made sacred. This attitude makes possible the kind of joy that endures hardship and the vacillating fortunes of life. This book explains the basic principles of being small and the practical skills to make everyday life sacred. These allow grace to come into our lives and bless us with happiness.

It is impossible to speak about this way without mentioning the everyday world we actually live in—a world plagued by complexity, strife, and darkness. To not address this would make our discussion abstract and antithetical to the way of the small, which by its very nature strives to embrace the details of daily existence. Our concern in this book will not be with specific events, such as 9/11 and its aftermath, but rather with the general problem of modern times. The principles for living small that promote a healthy, fruitful life for the individual can do the same for society, as they speak to the inflated or grandiose thinking that is responsible for many of our global problems. Perhaps the wisdom of living small can also help us deal with feeling overwhelmed and helpless.

The way of the small is not a theory, formula, or fixed belief system, but an organic way of living. My encounter with it naturally reflects my particular experience, and of course, the traditions and people I draw upon in the following pages bring their own perspectives. It is my hope that you may find a way into the small through *your* experience, experimenting to see for yourself if, indeed, very little is needed to make a happy life.

Part One

WHAT IS THE
WAY OF THE SMALL?

*A righteous man who was opposed to Rabbi Mendel of Kotzk
sent him a message: "I am so great that I reach into the seventh
firmament." The rabbi of Kotzk sent back his answer: "I am so
small that all the seven firmaments rest upon me."*

[HASIDIC TALE]

Though the mills of God grind slowly, they grind exceedingly small.

[WINSTON CHURCHILL]

CHAPTER ONE

A SMALL TALE

There once was a great king who died and went to the gate of heaven. He was expecting to see large pearly gates and St. Peter sitting on a throne. Instead he found Peter standing in front of a plain, small doorway.

"May I come in?" he asked the saint.

"Let's see," Peter said, looking over his notes. "It is true," he began, "that you were a great king with a great kingdom. Yes, you had many wives and children and much wealth, and made many important changes in the world. But you were larger than life. You yourself have become so identified with your crown of greatness that you would not know who you are without it. I'm afraid you won't fit in here. This place is small. You would not know how to live here. I'm sorry, you can't come in."

The king, shocked and dismayed, said, "What must I do to get in? I have nowhere to go."

"You do have some options," Peter said. "What I would suggest is that you go back to earth and learn to be small."

The king thought this over and, though not happy about it, decided it was acceptable. So Peter arranged for him to go back.

In his next life, the king purposely chose a path that was not so big. He returned to the kingdom and became a healer to the poor folk. He studied hard and became very knowledge-able and skilled. And he traveled far and wide healing many sick people. As he was much in demand, he did not have time to have a family, but this suited him fine—some of the kindred souls he met on his journeys became like family. Finally he reached old age, died, and once again found himself facing St. Peter at the gate of heaven.

He said to Peter, "I have lived a small life, helping others and sacrificing my own comfort. Can I now enter heaven?"

"Hmmm," St. Peter said, examining his revised notes. "I see that indeed you chose a smaller life, doing much good serv-ing others. But is it not true that you were also secretly very proud of this, feeling like you were on a heavenly mission and doing this mostly for your own salvation?"

"Well," the healer-king said, "what's wrong with that?"

"Nothing," Peter said, "but it's not small."

Upon hearing this the healer-king became furious, and started shouting obscenities at the old saint.

"That's not small either," Peter said.

"Well, what must I do!?" the healer-king asked in exas-peration.

"Try again," Peter said.

So the healer-king went back to earth, choosing this time a simple life as a shoemaker in a village at the outer edge of the kingdom. He married a village girl, raised a couple of children, and lived in a small cottage with his shoe shop attached. As the years went by he grew into a serene happiness, enjoying his family, his work, his neighbors. At the end of each day he loved to come into the living room of his home and spend the evenings with his family sharing stories in front of the fireplace. He grew to be very old in this life, surviving his wife and even his children. And although he was lonely, he still enjoyed his days, making shoes and sitting by the fireplace at night in contemplative reverie, as old men like to do.

Finally the old shoemaker died and was once again standing face to face with St. Peter at the gate of heaven.

"You know," he said before Peter could utter a word, "that was so good, you could send me back one more time."

St. Peter smiled. "Come in," he said.

CHAPTER TWO

WE ARE THE WAY OF THE SMALL

They asked Rabbi Aaron of Karlin what he had learned from his teacher, the Great Maggid. "Nothing at all," he said. And when they pressed him to explain what he meant by that, he added: "The nothing-at-all is what I learned. I learned the meaning of nothingness. I learned that I am nothing at all, and that I Am, notwithstanding."

[HASIDIC TALE]

THE SIGNIFICANCE OF OUR INSIGNIFICANCE

The universe is a vast, mysterious place. Clearly, we are very small in it, and, even with the advances of modern science, very limited in what we understand about it. And yet, in spite of this—or maybe because of it—we spend much time convincing ourselves and each other that we are anything *but* small and limited. Unlike other creatures, we are unusually preoccupied with our self-importance. How easily we get wounded or angry, for example, when someone attacks our self-image. Or how desperately we seek to assure some permanence from our life endeavors; something that lasts beyond us. Though we may profess one belief or another about an afterlife, we really don't know what will become of us. Our smallness is a perennial source of anguish, a constant reminder of our insignificance in the cosmic scheme of things. However, if we could only see that our smallness *is* what makes us great, perhaps we wouldn't need to *pretend* to be great by our inflation or grandiosity. Our significance would be discovered *in* the fleeting quality of life, not beyond it.

Some years ago I had an experience that shed some light on this matter, showing how an appreciation of our small-ness helps us live in a truly meaningful way. While visiting my brother and sister-in-law in Washington, D.C., I went to the United States Holocaust Memorial Museum. Although I had visited other Holocaust museums in the world, this was unlike any other exhibit, of *any* kind, that I had ever seen.

As you approach the museum, you are struck by the ar-chitecture that is modern and elegant but reminiscent of con-centration camp imagery: a guard tower hovering overhead, sentry boxes lining the roof, solid window panes you cannot see through. Heavy steel trusses above the Hall of Witness through which you enter the museum prepare your imagina-tion to confront the cold hard facts of one of history's dark-est episodes. The sculptures are stark, and the building's walls and windows impress upon you the sensation that you are in a prison.

The emaciated survivors and open mass graves of na-ked, starved, dead bodies are portrayed without apology in haunting black-and-white photographs taken by the Ameri-can liberation forces. From this end point you then go back to the very beginning, to see how it all began. You learn about the historical and cultural soil in which the seeds of Nazism grew. As you progress to Hitler's emergence on the scene and his takeover of Germany, you study the edicts that step-by-step built up a totalitarian state, first marginalizing and then criminalizing the Jews, Gypsies, and other groups of which German society needed to be "cleansed."

And then comes the war, with its systematic destruction of the Jews. You are flooded with news clippings, photographs, and audio and film recordings that show how the rich diversity of European Jewish family life was slowly decimated. A palpable feeling of depression—or is it oppression?—overcomes you from the pictures of some of the 400 ghettos in which they were interned. The barbed-wire fences, deteriorated, wintery surroundings, and long faces tell you of the subhuman conditions they lived in.

Now you come to the hundreds of forced-labor and concentration camps, with their rows and rows of barracks and the medical experiments on prisoners—starvation, freezing, and high-altitude experiments. Displays of experimental rooms, equipment, and a dissecting table send chills down your spine, especially when you are informed that children were subjects, too.

At last, you encounter the macabre reality of the "final solution"—the extermination camps. You begin with the mass-murder operations of the *Einsatzgruppen* (mobile killing units). You then learn about and see photographs of the four gas chambers at Auschwitz and the ovens used to burn the bodies. A scale model of Auschwitz's Crematorium II, with its tall, sturdy chimney, makes you reflect upon the skillful but wicked minds who designed this horror.

You walk by a small mountain of shoes from Jews who disappeared. You wonder, whose child did that little shoe over there belong to? You walk through a cattle car used in Poland during the war. You can't help but wonder: if not for the grace of God, you could have been in one of those cattle cars that freighted thousands—entire families together, but more often broken apart—to their deaths every day, indeed, like cattle.

The personal survivor accounts that are made available to you on audio assault your sensibilities and deliver a devastating blow to your wish to believe in the innate goodness of the human soul. By showing humanity's dark side, this museum provides a valuable service: it is both a reminder and a warning.

After eight hours on my feet, I not only felt as if the wind had been knocked out of me, but the spirit, too. The next day I was in no mood to go to another museum. I had been crushed by the weight of the exhibit, as if a truck had run over me. Naturally, I pondered such universal questions as, "What could be the purpose of such profound suffering?" and, "How could God allow it?" But these were not foremost in my mind. As important as they are, these questions seemed to be an escape from the raw reality of the suffering itself; they sought a way to cope with the suffering by framing it in a larger, religious context. I was gripped by the suffering and compelled to stay with it on its own terms, helpless and overwhelmed as this made me feel.

✻ ✻ ✻

Two days after the Holocaust excursion, I still wasn't particularly motivated, but decided to go to the Smithsonian's National Air and Space Museum. The museum was very crowded, and I found the long lines frustrating. I noticed an exhibit in a small movie theater that had no line. I was relieved to find that I was the only one there and sat down. As the lights dimmed, the title came on the screen: "POWERS OF TEN. A FILM DEALING WITH THE RELATIVE SIZE OF THINGS IN THE UNIVERSE AND THE EFFECT OF ADDING ANOTHER ZERO." The opening scene is a young couple having a picnic, with carnival music playing in the background. An announcer's voice comes on:

> *The picnic near the lakeside in Chicago is the start of a lazy afternoon early one October. We begin with a scene one meter wide which we view from just one meter away. Now every ten seconds we will look from ten times farther away and our field of view will be ten times wider.*

The camera begins to zoom out and upwards, giving the impression that we are looking down from an ascending rocket. In a few moments we cannot see the couple at all—only their blanket. Soon we see Chicago's Lake Shore Drive and Marina, the blanket barely a speck. As the camera continues, Lake Michigan comes into view, and then the entire Earth. Soon we see the moon orbiting the Earth, before passing the orbital paths of Venus, Mars, and Mercury. Then comes our glowing sun, followed by the wide orbital paths of the massive outer planets and Pluto.

As I watched our solar system merge indistinguishably with the myriad of stars in our galaxy, I could feel a strange nervousness in my heart, as if I were really "out there" on a voyage in outer space. "Good God!," I thought. "This is really far!"

As we traverse and exit our Milky Way galaxy, with its ten billion trillion stars and its glowing gas, it appears as a great flat spiral, like a hurricane photographed from a satellite. Its bright light dissipates into white clouds fanning out. It is awesome.

Passing the Clouds of Magellan and the big Virgo cluster of galaxies, our galaxy now looks small. Soon entire galaxies appear as single points of light. Reaching 100 million light years from the Earth, our voyage pauses briefly as we remain stationary in midspace. Galaxies are like dust in this rather empty, lonely scene. This emptiness, our announcer tells us, is what most of space normally looks like, the richness of our own neighborhood being the exception.

The feeling of nervousness has made way for what I can describe only as a "panic of the imagination." "What would happen," I asked myself, "if we didn't turn around as promised by the announcer? This universe is so immense that I'd never find my way back!" I could feel my heart sink as another thought forced its way into my mind. "Oh my God," I said to myself. "The Holocaust doesn't mean anything out here." This thought was not irrational. Think about it: From this vantage point in outer space, the Holocaust—indeed, all of human history, all of life on Earth, the Earth itself—is not even a blip on the screen. Whether or not the cries of six million reached God's heaven we can only guess, but for sure they didn't reach these heavens, barren and endlessly receding as they are. I had always known intellectually that the infinitude of the universe and the eternity of time made everything seem like nothing, and that the finitude of our planet and human species was as unavoidable as the finitude of our individual lives, but at this moment I knew it with a crisp, sensory certainty. Everything is nothing.

The return home is a sped-up version of the course we took to get here, taking but a fraction of the time (less than a minute). The announcer informs us that we will now go into the nucleus and proton of a carbon atom beneath the skin on the hand of the sleeping man at the picnic.

We slow down one meter from the picnic scene. We are told that we will reduce the distance to our destination 90 percent every ten seconds, each step much smaller than the one before. The structure of the skin becomes visible close-up. We enter the skin, crossing its layers into a tiny blood vessel. We encounter red and white blood cells. Crossing a white cell's porous wall, we penetrate its nucleus. Soon we see the coils of the DNA double helix molecule that contains the genetic code. Sizes are now measured in angstroms and nanometers.

Finally we reach the atomic scale, where we encounter the building blocks of DNA and focus on a carbon atom bonded to three hydrogen atoms. We cross through the shimmering, outer electron shell of the carbon atom to enter its center. Then we traverse a vast space of nothingness. At last, we arrive at the nucleus of the carbon atom. A structure of six protons and six neutrons, it is so massive and yet so small. We zoom in on a single proton.

Conceding that we have reached the edge of present scientific understanding, our announcer questions if what lies beyond is the realm of quarks. Our journey concluded, we are left with the striking realization of how immense the universe is on both macrocosmic and microcosmic levels.

* * *

The combination of the Holocaust museum and this short but powerful film stunned me: the intensely human, personal dimension of the museum and the impersonal dimension of the film met like two hands clapping loudly. Perhaps these were the two hands of God, one personal and the other impersonal, one connected to the moral dimension of good and evil and the other beyond it. The dilemma this duality raises, however, has as much to do with us as with God, since the one thing that is certain is that *we* have to bridge these two dimensions. *How do we live in a humanly meaningful and moral way while at the same time recognizing our utter insignificance in this vast universe?* This huge and thorny problem, a preoccupation of many religious and philosophical thinkers, came alive for me that day, and since then I have had a chance to reflect on it from the viewpoint of the way of the small.

To begin, the way of the small shows what is truly significant, or at least it puts our human significance on a level playing field with our cosmic insignificance. It is precisely because human life is such a rarity in this vast and seemingly lifeless universe that it is so significant. Whether or not you believe in God, life on Earth is a miracle. The statistical chances against its emergence are as vast as the cosmos. From a cosmic stand-point, life itself is the way of the small, as is the fact that it evolved on an infinitesimally little planet spinning around an infinitesimally small star at the edge of an infinitesimal galaxy in the middle of nowhere. What a precious anomaly and exception to the cosmic rule!

If the way of the small casts a different light upon my museum visits, as just described, what light in return do the visits shed upon the way of the small? The exhibits I saw tell us that our humanity and inhumanity take place in an extremely small slice of the cosmos. This slice is between the macrocosmic and the microcosmic, between that infinite realm "out there" and that infinitesimal realm "in there." Events like the picnic in Chicago and the Holocaust both happen in this small slice; they have no meaning "out there" beyond the Milky Way and "in there" at the atomic level. To embrace the way of the small in this context does not mean to be as small as possible, for as we see, the smallness of the microcosmic is actually quite immense and ungraspable. Embracing smallness here means inhabiting the smallness that is ours as fully as possible. It means fully inhabiting the small slice of the cosmos we live in. This is where all meaning and morality exist. This alone is the human dimension.

When we begin to examine this small slice of the cosmos we live in, this human dimension, we see that it is a small universe in its own right, with its own rules or laws that have absolute significance for its sustenance. One of those rules or laws, curiously, is that we give our lives absolute or objective significance. Without this, meaning and morality could not exist, and life would become intolerable, as the Holocaust demonstrated only too well. In this, as in so many other matters, the way of the small goes *with* the force of nature, not against it. Nature (or evolution) has endowed us with the conviction that we and our survival are important. This conviction is rooted in both our egos and our instincts. (Animals appear to share the same conviction but on a purely instinctual, pre-egoistic level.) Certainly, for our survival and physical and mental health, we need to feel that we are important. Otherwise we may lose our interest in life.

From this standpoint, our self-importance is absolutely real. Being not only natural but necessary, a *proper* sense of self-importance is part of the way of the small. This is not to put a different spin on our cosmic insignificance, which the way of the small also appreciates by its very focus on our smallness. Merely, this is to acknowledge that our significance is absolute in our small slice of the cosmos as much as our insignificance is absolute in the cosmos at large. We are both absolutely important *and* absolutely unimportant. As the physicist Niels Bohr said, "The opposite of a profound truth may well be another profound truth."

So, how do we live in a humanly meaningful and moral way while at the same time recognizing our utter insignificance in this vast universe? The way of the small instructs us to *own* our smallness by keeping our eyes on the stars but our feet on the ground. That ground is our human existence and humanity. To own or inhabit our smallness means to squarely and honestly accept our unimportance in the cosmic scheme of things while honoring our importance in the human scheme of things. Paradoxical as it may sound, recognizing our unimportance and wearing it like a badge of courage may be the single-most important, meaningful thing we ever do in our quest to find our place in this vast and lonely cosmos.

As I am writing these words on my yellow notepad, a small spider has come out of nowhere and is boldly walking across it, as if to say, "Here I am." I wonder: Where did she come from? Where is she going? She seems very intent on getting there. Her purpose, however, is significant only to her. In my world, a much larger universe than hers, it makes no real difference where she is going and what she will do when she gets there. Her doings have as much bearing upon my world as mine do upon the infinite universe beyond my own. Yet a thought stirs within me as I watch her walk away: my yellow pad will suddenly seem like a lonely, lifeless thing without her. I suppose I and my larger universe should thank her for visiting.

The way of the small holds together the opposites of our unimportance and importance. We are, like this little spider, unimportant and important at the same time. By going into our smallness as fully as possible, we discover our true place and significance in the universe: *Here we are.*

POTENT QUOTES

It is very hard to realize that [the Earth] is just a tiny part of an overwhelmingly hostile universe. It is even harder to realize that this present universe has evolved from an unspeakably unfamiliar early condition, and faces a future extinction of endless cold or intolerable heat. The more the universe seems comprehensible, the more it also seems pointless. But if there is no solace in the fruits of our research, there is at least some consolation in the research itself. . . . The effort to understand the universe is one of the very few things that lifts human life a little above the level of farce, and gives it some of the grace of tragedy.

[STEVEN WEINBERG]

We are just an advanced breed of monkeys on a minor planet of a very average star. But we can understand the Universe. That makes us something very special.

[STEPHEN HAWKING]

With all its sham, drudgery, and broken dreams, it is still a beautiful world.

[MAX EHRMANN]

CHAPTER THREE

GOD'S SMALL SECRET

*And behold, the Lord passed by, and a great and strong wind tore
into the mountains and broke the rocks in pieces before the Lord,
but the Lord was not in the wind; and after the wind an
earthquake, but the Lord was not in the earthquake; and
after the earthquake a fire, but the Lord was not in the fire;
and after the fire a still small voice.*

[1 KINGS 19:11-12]

A SLICE OF SMALLNESS

Edith Reich, a Hungarian Jewish Holocaust survivor, tells
the following story about an experience in the war:

During the last year of the war I was running for my
life with illegal identification papers, without any real
connections to the underground. I was struggling to
just survive from one day to the next, one hour to
the next. The city of Budapest was under siege for
months. The Germans were holding it, and we were
surrounded by the Red Army. In the mornings the
British bombed the city; at night, the Americans. The

Russians bombed all day and all night. For months nobody could remain at home. Everyone moved down to the underground bomb shelters and lived there permanently. People only went out on the streets when necessary, to take care of basic survival needs (food, hospital, etc.).

I was hiding in a store on street level. The windows were covered with wood panels. I could not have the luxury to go down and join people in the shelters in case there would be a search by the Germans or the Hungarian fascists. (They were looking not only for Jews, but deserters.) I was somehow never afraid of the terrible bombings. My friend who owned the store could not get over how I could stand it. He was living in a shelter, and came to the store basically for my sake to bring me some food and hot tea with schnapps. He would open the shop every morning at 10:00 for an hour or two, then close it, come back in the afternoon and open it again for an hour or so, and finally close it at 4:00. He thought it was a miracle that I was never afraid, since the people below were terrified.

Early one morning in January, at about 5:00, I woke up. It was as if a small voice had whispered into my ear, "Get out of this building." It left me with a terrible panicky feeling. I promised myself I would get out of here the minute my friend would come and open the store. I was praying—shaking with fear—the whole time until 10:00.

When my friend came, I told him what happened to me. He had some similar experiences with me before, and I think he believed a little bit that I had a guardian angel of some sort. He said, "Relax now, drink some hot tea with schnapps, and then we'll go. Somebody will make a place for you downstairs in the shelter." I was ready to go, my few belongings packed since the early morning when I had been awakened. I said that I didn't want tea or anything, just to get out of here right away. So we went, carrying my belongings.

We came out of the store and started towards the shelter. Suddenly there was a terribly loud and powerful detonation. We fell down, all black from the dirt and smoke. The front of the store had been hit by a Russian bomb. Everything was blown to pieces.

My friend told me later that not only had he saved my life by letting me hide in his store (thus endangering his own life), but I saved his, too. Yet I feel that it was not me, but an invisible power that saved us. Time and time again during these final months of the war, just minutes before peril, this power would save me.

THE ABSOLUTELY SMALL

What is the nature of God? This has been a burning question ever since man first became aware that there may be an intelligence beyond his own. Of course, the answer to this metaphysical question is unknowable with any degree of certainty.

But perhaps what traditional religion tells us about the ways God works—the *size* of his manifestations—can shed some light on his nature.

Traditional religion tells us that God likes the way of the small. It is true that, according to the Bible, God undertook a colossal act in creating the universe, and then often intervened in magnificent and diverse ways in human affairs. But as time went on, his role in the world has seemed to get progressively smaller, to the point that today he seems entirely hidden, as if he has gone into retreat. Mystics retreating into the desert and caves and monasteries do so because they know that God can best be seen in the quiet of the night and the interior world. There is much to suggest that by choice, he is not as almighty as we might think. The Book of Genesis explicitly shows that after the first six days of creation, God did not have control over where it was going or how its human inhabitants behaved. The Talmud pointedly tells us that because God has foreknowledge of the future does not mean he controls it or that we do not possess free will. And St. Augustine, too, was clear on the mysterious role of God in history: that God is active in history as the redeemer does not imply that he runs it according to a bureaucratic master plan.

Another theological idea holds that God began the universe with a single act that set everything in motion, and then he let the rest take its course. This would then be a universe that has a divine origin but unfolds of its own accord in a more-or-less spontaneous, unpredictable fashion—even from God's standpoint. (This leaves no question about the existence of free will.) Science even enriches this view by suggesting that the universe unfolds by way of the small. Darwin's theory of evolution asserts that species evolve by making many adaptations and that countless species have gone extinct. The rather blind and mechanistic process of this led Darwin to argue against any purpose of intelligence inherent within evolution other than the survival of the fittest. Though he was unsure about God's existence, he was certain that he had no role in evolution. But the way of the small did: "Natural selection can act only by the preservation and accumulation of infinitesimally small inherited modifications, each profitable to the preserved being [that is, species]." Perhaps God created the universe and then set it on its course through the workings of the small.

More recently, Big Bang theorists like Georges Lemaître and Edwin Hubble also conjectured that the cosmos began with an original causal event. The fact that they can agree on no single scenario of how it will unfold indicates that they, too, do not see evidence of an intelligent plan. For them, the cosmos *began* small. Prior to the Big Bang it was, as Lemaître described it, a "primeval atom" with all the energy and mass of the universe condensed in it. Approximately 10^{-34} seconds after the Big Bang it was merely the size of a marble. As for the process that *formed* the cosmos, chaos theory shows how small changes can have large effects. For example, the "Butterfly Effect" states that, in theory, the flutter of a butterfly's wings in China can set off a chain of events affecting weather patterns in the United States. Chaos theory proposes that cosmic processes, though following physical law, are so complex that they are indistinguishable from what we would classify as random. In short, the "big boss" theory of God is unfounded in both science and religion.

So what then is the nature or role of God in the cosmos? The above notions seem to require of us a simple, implicit trust that the universe "happens" by itself. For all its evolutionary extinctions, seemingly random occurrences, and human acts of folly and evil that give it a bad name, the cosmos essentially must have God's blessing even if he is not running it as a "big boss." Otherwise, could it exist? "The world is its own magic," the Zen master Shunryu Suzuki said. This means that the divine nature of the world is not apparent in a grand way, or what we suppose is a grand way. It is apparent in small ways. The way of the small appears to be one vital way that God's blessings and presence manifest in the world. If this is so, perhaps God is closer and more attainable than we think. We merely look for him in the wrong places and in the wrong ways.

JUDAISM

The world's great religions do more than show the historical roots of the way of the small. They abundantly confirm God's own preference for smallness, though one needs a special eye to see this preference. Even the proclamations of the way of the small are small, often going unnoticed for what they are. One example of this is the Hebrew Bible's description of the ark that contained the Ten Commandments and served as the meeting place for God and the high priest. This ark was a rectangular chest the size of a small trunk. God would speak to the high priest from a point between two gold-sculpted angels who were part of the throne that was on top of this chest. The Bible here almost makes it sound like God *himself* is small, or at least can *become* small:

> There I shall come to meet you; there, from above the throne of mercy, from between the two cherubs that are on the ark of the Testimony, I shall give you all my commands for the sons of Israel.

These commands—613 of them including the Ten Commandments—constitute the Mosaic Law. A comprehensive guide to daily living, they make the ordinary sacred by giving special importance to even the smallest concern, whether in matters of worship, diet, sex, civil penalties, or taxes.

Judaism's later emphasis upon ethics, education, and family life further embodied the divine in the world through the small. The Talmud is famous not only for its scholarly elucidation of Mosaic Law, but its wisdom. Many of its teachings mirror what it means to live small. "Who is wealthy?" the Talmudic Fathers ask. "He who is content with what he has."

In Jewish mysticism we see yet another illustration of the way of the small. According to the Kabbalistic idea of creation, God firstly had to withdraw and contract into himself to provide a space for the universe. Because God is everywhere, in all things and all places, a primordial space that would allow creation's independence had to be established. Naturally, his divine presence remained in creation, but in a subtle, hidden way. This notion of God making himself small is known as *tzim tzum*. Secondly, the divine light which is the essence of God was at a certain moment shattered out of its original condition, falling into exile as a myriad of small sparks. These became the cosmos, including our souls and bodies. This is one of the ways God's presence is in creation. The sparks inhabit all things, trapped in them. Through righteous deeds and intentions, the Kabbalist's goal is to free and raise these sparks to the higher world from which they came and reunite them again into the original, single flame of God. This repairing of our world, known as *tikkun olam*, will redeem *both* man *and* God. According to this view, not only does God manifest through the small, but the way of the small transforms the divine-human drama.

CHRISTIANITY

Christianity has its own distinct approach to the way of the small. When Jesus proclaimed that "the kingdom of God is within you," he meant that the divine could be encountered directly and not just through the Mosaic Law. This direct cultivation of the kingdom of God is the way of the small. "Whoever becomes small shall understand the kingdom," Jesus tells us in the Gospel of Thomas. Elsewhere, in one of his most famous parables, he explains that "The kingdom of heaven is like a grain of mustard seed which a man took and sowed in his field; it is the smallest of all seeds, but when it has grown it is the greatest of shrubs and becomes a tree, so that the birds of the air come and make nests in its branches." In other words, heaven grows in our hearts and minds from small beginnings. This is how God brings about great and lasting changes.

Many of Jesus' teachings further illustrate his approach to cultivating the small. When he said, "Except ye be converted, and become as little children, ye shall not enter into the kingdom of heaven," he was encouraging us to be child*like*— to appreciate each day anew, each event with open and alert eyes, each thing as an invitation to participate in the mystery and joy of creation. We must become small as a child to grasp the small, miraculous wonders of life. He similarly warns us about becoming too big or encumbered with attachments: "It is easier for a camel to go through the eye of a needle than for a rich man to enter the kingdom of God." When Jesus instructed us to have a faith that does not demand sensational demonstrations of God's existence—miracles—he was also speaking to the small: God manifests in subtle ways. And when he advised us to be like the birds and the lilies of the field, he was telling us to be like God's other creatures who naturally practice the way of the small, living in the here-and-now without anxiety.

Jesus' life is an example of the way of the small. He came onto the scene not as a vociferous opponent of the Roman regime, but as a gentle reformer of the inner life ("Render to Caesar the things that are Caesar's, and to God the things that are God's"). He kept company with the lowly—lepers, prostitutes, and other outcasts—practicing his own teaching that "he who is least among you all is the one who is great." And he died the death of a common criminal, himself diminished, disregarded, and anguished. "My God, my God, why hast thou forsaken me?": what could be a more poignant expression of feeling small? Jesus' "poverty of spirit"—in fact a richness because of its simplicity—was a living demonstration of the way of the small, and has been emulated by Christian mystics through the centuries.

ISLAM

Islam is very much the way of the great, with its song of praise about God's power and glory and the Koran's words that tell us "Whichever way you turn, there is the face of Allah." However, at a closer look, we see that the way of the small is found in Islam's *response* to divine greatness. This takes the form of submitting to God's will (the Arabic word *islam* literally means "submission"). Two of the more obvious acts that convey this submission are removing one's shoes upon entering the mosque and kneeling in prayer. One humbly bows down and acknowledges one's smallness in the face of God's greatness. More central are the Five Pillars of Islam: (1) giving testimony of one's faith in God and Muhammad as his prophet; (2) performance of ritual prayers five times a day; (3) self-purification through fasting during the month of Ramadan; (4) giving alms to the needy; and (5) making a pilgrimage to Mecca if one is able. This precise structuring of life makes Islam as much a way of the small as of the great.

The mystical Sufis place special emphasis on the way of the small. Their literature shows the importance of humility in assisting Allah in his effort to bestow upon the world his most precious gift, mercy. The Sufi dervishes physically enact the way of the small through their ritual dance. The dance is conceived as a doorway to paradise, to ecstasy and union with God. It opens a small passageway between the material and spiritual, heavenly worlds. Its small, whirling circles and the small, controlled movements of hands, head, and arms suggest that being small in the way we live is essential for passing through this doorway.

TAOISM

The way of the small is perhaps more clearly articulated in Eastern religions, as Taoism illustrates. This tradition is very forthright in its belief that the Tao or Way, the central organizing principle of life, is as much the way of the small as the way of the great. Yet from a human standpoint (in contrast to the cosmic one), the small is preferred. The student of the Tao is encouraged to follow the great, but be the small. (The Western analogy is, "Keep your eyes on the stars but your feet on the ground.") In the *Tao Te Ching*, Taoism's core scripture, Lao-tzu states:

> *The Great Tao flows everywhere.*
> *It may go left or right.*
> *All things depend on it for life, and it does not turn away from them.*
> *It accomplishes its task, but does not claim credit for it.*
> *It clothes and feeds all things but does not claim to be master over them.*
> *Always without desires, it may be called The Small.*

> *All things come to it and it does not master them; it may be called The Great.*
> *Therefore (the sage) never strives himself for the great, and thereby the great is*
>   *achieved.*

In other words, it is through the small that greatness is achieved. "Small" and "great" were actually the original meanings, respectively, of yin and yang.

Also to be expected, Taoism advocates modest behavior that adheres to the way of the small:

> *. . . let people hold on to these:*
> *Manifest plainness,*
> *Embrace simplicity,*
> *Reduce selfishness,*
> *Have few desires.*

The way of the small is the way into the Tao.

CONFUCIANISM

Even fortune cookies quoting Confucius often demonstrate that Confucianism is a tradition firmly rooted in the way of the small. Its text *The Doctrine of the Mean* makes this way its main theme. It establishes the "middle way"—an ethical balance between the extremes of being amoral and too moral, or indulgent and puritanical—as a compass for the good life and a guideline for moral action. The Confucian equivalent of Aristotle's Golden Mean, the middle way advocates living with limits and balance in a range of matters, including love.

Confucius here differed from Jesus. Asked once if we should love our enemy and those who harm us, he replied, "By no means. Answer hatred with justice and love with benevolence. Otherwise you would waste your benevolence."

Confucianism is very much a religion of ethics and expresses the way of the small with a keen attention to the details of being a moral and socially responsible person. The development of personal character—particularly *jen* or good-heartedness—is of primary importance. Confucius honored the small when he shifted Chinese religion's focus upon Heaven to Earth ("Heaven" understood here as the realm of the ancestors and Shang Ti, the supreme ancestor or deity). This change placed man and his small world upon center stage. Although Confucius still had a profound belief in the power of Heaven's will or "Mandate," this allowed him to develop his practical, worldly philosophy. All things small and human became worthy of his wise scrutiny.

Confucius says: "Small is the cooing dove, but it flies aloft to Heaven."

* * *

Originating centuries prior to Taoism and Confucianism and a source of inspiration for both is the *I Ching* or *Book of Changes*. Eventually considered one of the five great Confucian classics, the *I Ching* is not only a book of Chinese philosophy, but an oracle that is used to divine the underlying principles that shape present situations. Jung became interested in it for this ability to access the unconscious or unseen dimension of things. The *I Ching* consists of 64 hexagrams or ideographic symbols depicting situations we commonly find ourselves in during the course of our lives. The situations are presented with gentle advice on how to respond to them in a way that promotes harmony, positive change, or acceptance.

Two hexagrams that directly point to the way of the small are "The Taming Power of the Small" and "Preponderance of the Small." The first of these states that the force of the small brings success even in situations where there is little room for movement. By taming and applying our energy in a disciplined way, we make the most of it. The ancient Chinese understood that the world can be transformed through a steady process of small changes. The modern Chinese draw from such wisdom in their heritage when they say they are an old civilization that knows how to be patient and build slowly but surely toward the future. Indeed, the Chinese attained their status as a 3700-year-old civilization in no small measure by practicing the way of the small.

Likewise, in "Preponderance of the Small," we are encouraged to give the way of the small a prevalent role in our everyday lives. The *I Ching* translator Richard Wilhelm here comments that the superior or wise person is

> exceptionally conscientious in his actions. In bereavement emotion means more to him than ceremoniousness. In all his personal expenditures he is extremely simple and unpretentious. In comparison with the man of the masses, all this makes him stand out as exceptional. But the essential significance of his attitude lies in the fact that in external matters he is on the side of the lowly.

Even the hexagrams "The Taming Power of the Great" and "Preponderance of the Great" promote the way of the small as the best means for managing great enterprises or endeavors. They suggest that in our greatness, too, we should exercise modesty, self-restraint, and a reliance on inner worth rather than external brilliance.

HINDUISM

A colorful, complex tradition, Hinduism offers much in the way of the small. Its mythic stories, philosophy, religious practices, and modern applications (such as the political protest of Gandhi) all embody the way of the small. The religion's polytheism and pantheism parade the Absolute in its smaller manifestations. In Hinduism, there is no distinct, monumental beginning of creation. Brahman or God resides in the universe, dwelling in each thing and person as a spark of divinity.

In its human form, Brahman is referred to as the *atman*, or the eternal, inner self. This is the principle or entity that gives man his essential nature. Because the *atman* is a localized form of God—complete in itself, self-dependent, wise, and immortal—the person who knows it has no fear of death. He knows that the small is identical to the "All," and that the inner self is identical to the self of God. The *Katha Upanishad* states:

> Smaller than the small, greater than the great, the self is set in the heart of every creature. The unstriving man beholds Him, freed from sorrow. Through tran-

quillity of mind and the senses he sees the greatness of the self.

"Smaller than the small" means that the *atman* is smaller than an atom. Elsewhere in the *Upanishads* the *atman* is described as the "person of the size of a thumb [who] resides in the middle of the body" and as the "dwarf who is seated in the middle." These references to the middle of the body signify the heart.

Westerners who practice yoga know that it is a discipline of the small. Hatha or physical yoga cultivates the way of the small with its many precise postures, controlled movements, and attention to small, subtle details of the body. Perhaps Hinduism's most sublime yet simple expression of the way of the small is the *Bhagavad Gita*, a small piece of scripture inserted into the *Mahabharata* epic at its most dramatic point. It advocates the path of yoga and the value of nonattachment, advising us to renounce the fruits of our actions to God. This is less about asceticism than about making everyday life sacred by dedicating what we do to God. One can see why the *Bhagavad Gita*, in extolling renunciation and selflessness as the way to be small, became Gandhi's bible.

BUDDHISM

Buddhism's love of the small is well-known: minimalism is intrinsic to its philosophy. Buddha himself, like Jesus, lived a life that epitomized the way of the small. He started off as a prince and ended as a beggar who died from food poisoning. His central teaching is very straightforward and simple: life is full of suffering; the cause of suffering is craving; and to cease suffering, one must give up craving. These are the first three of the Four Noble Truths. The Fourth Noble Truth consists of the Eightfold Path. This is Buddha's strategy for living small, "strategy" understood here as a specific application of principles or skills. The Eightfold Path focuses on a specific end in a specific manner: In order to abolish suffering and its roots in craving, one must cultivate (1) right understanding, (2) right intention, (3) right speech, (4) right conduct, (5) right livelihood, (6) right effort, (7) right mindfulness, and (8) right concentration. To be free from suffering does not mean that we no longer experience the natural pain of living and dying. Rather, the desire to escape that pain through all the things we crave is sacrificed, thereby eliminating the human component that makes our suffering so full of anguish.

Zen Buddhism in particular, with its premise that one can find the universe in a teacup, has fine-tuned the appreciation of the small. Zen arts such as tea ceremony, flower arrangement, and archery discipline the mind to grasp not only detail, but "suchness": just this moment, just this thing, exactly as it is, this is the fullness of life, this is the universe. The discovery of Buddha-nature, as this is also called, is not something otherworldly, but very much of this world. It *is* this world, but in its true nature as opposed to the way we think it is in our conditioned frame of mind. The concentration or "one-pointedness of mind" that is cultivated in Zen art and meditation shatters that frame of mind. It focuses the mind like a laser beam that pierces Buddha-nature. This is the small penetrating the great, and the ultimate inhabiting the small.

Perhaps more than any other school of Buddhism, Zen portrays the realization of Buddha-nature, or enlightenment, as a state of emptiness. This is not the nihilistic nothingness of existentialism, but a pregnant emptiness. One may experience it when the small becomes so small that it no longer even exists. Even the sense of oneself as an observer of this experience and the act of observing it have been extinguished. Sekito Kisen, an eighth century Chinese Zen master and poet, describes this experience:

> *I have built a strawroof hut where nothing is of value.*
> *After eating, I relax and take a nap.*
> *When the hut was finished, shoots appeared.*
> *Now weeds cover everything.*

> *The man in the hut lives peacefully, without ties inside*
>   *or outside. . . .*
> *Though this hut is small, it contains the universe.*
> *In ten square feet, an old man enlightens forms and their essence.*

"Though this hut is small, it contains the universe." What can better illustrate Buddhism's veneration of the way of the small, or for that matter, the veneration all the above religions express? After all, the idea that the infinite can be found in the small is a universal truth they all share.

POTENT QUOTES

[God] needs limitation in time and space. Let us therefore be for him limitation in time and space, an earthly tabernacle.

[C.G. JUNG]

How happy is the little Stone
That rambles in the Road alone,
And doesn't care about Careers
And Exigencies never fears—
Whose Coat of elemental Brown
A passing Universe put on,
And independent as the Sun
Associates or glows alone,
Fulfilling absolute Decree
In casual simplicity.

[EMILY DICKINSON]

To see a World in a grain of sand,
And a Heaven in a wild flower,
Hold Infinity in the palm of your hand,
And Eternity in an hour.

[WILLIAM BLAKE]

Part Two

ESSENTIAL PRINCIPLES FOR LIVING SMALL

The pursuit of Tao is to decrease day after day.
It is to decrease and further decrease until one reaches the point
of taking no action.
No action is undertaken, and yet nothing is left undone.

[LAO-TZU]

What we choose to fight is so tiny!
What fights with us is so great!
If only we would let ourselves be dominated
as things do by some immense storm,
we would become strong too, and not need names.

When we win it's with small things,
and the triumph itself makes us small.

[RAINER MARIA RILKE]

CHAPTER FOUR

BUILDING A FOUNDATION
FOR SUCCESS

In reading the lives of great men, I found that the first victory they won
was over themselves . . . self-discipline with all of them came first.

[HARRY S. TRUMAN]

The goal is to make the ego as strong and as small as possible.

[C.G. JUNG]

A SLICE OF SMALLNESS

In 1946, the *Chicago Tribune* printed a cartoon of President Harry S. Truman in which he was depicted as Little Lord Fauntleroy—the boy in Frances Hodgson Burnett's novel with the same name—being bullied by a gang of tough street kids labeled "Labor," "Management," "Party Radical," "Party Conservative," and "Foreign Diplomacy." Truman was often underestimated by the media and others as a "little man"—simple, unsophisticated, unable to rise to the challenges of the presidency. Commenting on his image as a fumbler, another newspaper cartoon had the caption, "To err is Truman." Through the lens of history, however, we can today more clearly see that Truman was among the great presidents and statesmen of the world. His greatness very much came from his *smallness*.

In his life as a public servant as well as in his personal affairs, Truman was on the side of the small—simple but not simple-minded, quiet-spoken and plain-spoken, down-to-earth and even-tempered, comfortable with himself, and modest to the point of self-effacing. "I shall attempt to meet your expectations," he humbly told one audience, "but do not expect too much of me." He stood against what he called the "dangers of bigness" in business—big banks, big insurance companies, big corporations, big unions—in which the control of wealth or power was concentrated in a few hands. Truman never wanted or set out to be president, preferring his position in the Senate. He fell into the presidency almost by accident—he was forced into it, as he saw it—and he always presented himself as an ordinary man needing the help of not only his advisors and family but every citizen ("I have the job and I have to do it and the rest of you have to help me").

Truman's approach to international affairs was a salute to the way of the small. After the defeat of Germany, he wrote that the three great powers must earn the confidence of "the *smaller* nations [emphasis his own]." In Truman's thinking, even his epoch-making decision to use the atomic bomb was an attempt to be as small as possible given the circumstances: in his radio address after the second bomb was dropped, he told the American people, "We have used it in order to shorten the agony of war, in order to save the lives of thousands and thousands of young Americans." Truman believed that forcing Japan to surrender quickly would also reduce *its* casualties. After the war, his policy of containment of the Soviets as an alternative to war shaped American foreign policy for the next half-century, and played a vital role in positioning America to eventually win the Cold War.

Truman understood that being small and strong were synonymous. Advised to name the Marshall Plan after himself—to follow suit with the Truman Doctrine—he insisted on giving the credit to whom he felt it really belonged. More than once he remarked how much could be accomplished if you didn't care who received the credit. Secretary of State Dean Acheson noted that "He was not afraid of the competition of other ideas. . . . Free of the greatest vice in a leader, his ego never came between him and his job." Historian David McCullough offers this assessment of Truman:

> Ambitious by nature, he was never torn by ambition, never tried to appear as something he was not. He stood for common sense, common decency. He spoke the common tongue. As much as any president since Lincoln, he brought to the highest office the language and values of the common American people. He held to the old guidelines: work hard, do your best, speak the truth, assume no airs, trust in God, have no fear. . . . He was the kind of president the founding fathers had in mind for the country. He came directly from the people. He *was* America.

LESS IS MORE, SIMPLER IS BETTER

How can we cultivate smallness? There is no single answer to this, since everyone must find their own way into the small. But there do seem to be some basic, universal principles or skills which give the way of the small its legs and make it an art of the possible.

Although it flies in the face of the American Dream or credo, *less is more, simpler is better* is probably the best-known principle for living small. The American ethos—in business and industry, in geopolitics, and in the personal sphere—is "more, more, more." More money, more things that money buys, more status, more power, more youth, glamour, and beauty. We have become consumers of happiness. As Joni Mitchell said, "Happiness is a good face lift." Today we see the result of a purely one-sided, materialistic understanding of happiness: America is the richest nation on earth with possibly the highest rate of clinical depression and anxiety.

The drive for "more, more, more" clearly plays a part in this. Affluence itself is not the problem; the ancients also valued material prosperity. The problem is the relentless pursuit of prosperity without regard for the spiritual side of life and the inability to find satisfaction with what one has. Henry David Thoreau, one of America's great masters of the way of the small, devoted his life to exploring a spiritual alternative to our materialistic culture. His approach to life was an experiment in "thrift" as this has always been understood: to be frugal *and* to thrive. Describing the quintessential Thoreau, his friend Ralph Waldo Emerson said, "To him, there was no such thing as size.

The pond was a small ocean, the Atlantic, a large Walden Pond." Jungian analyst Gilda Frantz characterizes Thoreau's thought as a philosophy of the small. His core belief, she writes, was that "In the observation of the small, life's larger issues are seen." Thoreau was convinced that to truly understand anything, it must be appreciated in its particular details. His fourteen-volume journal is a day-by-day, in-the-moment account of his life in the woods right down to its finest details.

When Thoreau said, "Simplicity, simplicity, simplicity!" he meant that life should be lived close to nature, to the basic eternal principles that shape all things. Whether discovered through philosophy or in nature itself, these provide a compass for the good life. But they have become obscured by the busy-ness of modern society, so that we no longer know how to live in harmony with nature or with our own true nature. Thoreau saw modern man's large ambitions, rapid pace of life, and technological gains as defensive shields against the vital force of life, and he strove to reach behind these to taste this force in its pure form:

> I went to the woods because I wished to live deliberately, to front only the essential facts of life, and see if I could not learn what it had to teach, and not, when I came to die, discover that I had not lived. I did not wish to live what was not life, living is so dear; nor did I wish to practise resignation, unless it was quite necessary. I wanted to live deep and suck out all the marrow of life, to live so sturdily and Spartan-like as to put to rout all that was not life, to cut a broad swath

and shave close, to drive life into a corner, and reduce it to its lowest terms, and, if it proved to be mean, why then to get the whole and genuine meanness of it, and publish its meanness to the world; or if it were sublime, to know it by experience, and be able to give a true account of it in my next excursion.

To "front only the essential facts of life," to "drive life into a corner, and reduce it to its lowest terms": *that* is the way of the small. Thoreau's humanity—his spirituality, philosophy, social views, and concern for fellow human and animal creatures alike—was deeply informed by this way of living that he practiced not as a master but a student, perpetually enchanted and surprised.

The point here is not to imitate Thoreau, to cultivate the small by going into the woods and living a life of austerity. We must each find our own path to simplicity by asking, "How is my life overly complicated? Where is it 'too much'? Are my days too crowded or rushed, and if so, how can I change this? Do I take one step at a time, one day at a time, or is my mind so busy planning the future that I do not savor what is immediately in front of me?" Less is more, simpler is better can take many forms, and needs to be tailored to whatever the forest of our individual lives looks like.

A psychotherapy patient whom we will call Jacob illustrates this point. (Henceforth as well, all patients will be referred to pseudonymously.) Jacob was in his early 30s. A highly successful corporate executive and vice president of a prestigious, national retail company, he was living the American Dream. He was also very driven and competitive, suffering from stress and anxiety, gambling with significant losses, and estranged from his wife. At one point he expanded his company beyond its means to cover its expenses, and nearly went bankrupt. Even though he had a beautiful house, he bought a new and bigger one on the grounds that it would be an improvement. Straining his assets and putting him into debt, this added more stress to his life. Finally in one session we had a discussion about happiness and the value of being small. I explained that happiness depends as much on saying "No" to the things we don't want in our lives as saying "Yes" to the things we do. When we clearly see their cost, money the least of it, we realize that the things we often *think* we want, we really don't. To "be small" here does not mean to be petty or narrow-minded, but to be uninflated and true to who we really are and our values. As an exercise for our next meeting, I asked Jacob to write a contemplative piece on what being small would look like in three areas of his life—his inner world, his work, and his marriage. He wrote:

Being Small on an Inner Level

Being small means knowing myself. It means being aware of my weaknesses and limitations. Being small means allowing myself to get to know others. It means allowing others to be better, brighter and more charming than me and appreciating their differences. Being small means allowing myself to be loved—both by others and myself. It means sharing my strengths and weaknesses, and allowing myself to be human.

Being Small in My Work

Being small in work means needing others. It means being able to depend on others. Being small can at times mean being weak, not knowing all the answers, or being unmotivated and unproductive. It means not always being in a rush. Being small can also simply mean being humble—which in fact is big—very big. It means being content and understanding your inner center.

Being Small in My Marriage

Being small in my marriage means letting go of my expectations. It means relinquishing my previous notions of marriage which were created through my role models/parents. Being small means listening and being patient. It means being able to say "I'm sorry" and truly mean it. It means trying to learn from my mistakes. Most importantly, being small means being small—that is, sharing the fact that I am small.

Focusing on essentials, these words aptly portray the spirit of less is more, simpler is better.

BEING ORDINARY BUT EXCEPTIONAL

The theologian Malcolm Spicer once said, "The mystical is not extraordinary. It is ordinary—very ordinary. The problem is that people do not experience the ordinary." The same thing is true about the way of the small. It is ordinary. Mystics such as St. Francis of Assisi and St. John of the Cross purposely sought to live very ordinary lives because, like Thoreau, they knew that the great truths of life are discovered by living small. Many Christian mystics went barefoot for this reason; this reminded them to be simple. Similarly, life in Zen monasteries aims to cultivate the ordinary and small. As the film *Enlightenment Guaranteed* illustrates, in Zen training, when you finish cleaning the floor and a cat comes along with dirty paws, you just start over. You don't get angry and curse the cat or your bad luck. The cleaning and sweeping in Zen monasteries is not about cleaning in itself or getting rid of dirt. It's about cleansing your heart and sweeping away your fears.

Living an ordinary life through the way of the small means being singularly focused on what life presents you. One does not need to be in a Zen monastery to be like this. Zen itself teaches that "true Zen does not smell of Zen." In the monastery-without-walls—the modern, secular, urban world in which most of us live—we can also do our "cleaning" and "sweeping" through our daily responsibilities. The challenge is perhaps more difficult: the demands of modern city life are often far from simple. But still, we can try to perform our tasks with an attitude that we are doing them simply for their own sake. This consecrates or makes sacred the ordinary.

Some years ago, a bright young woman came to see me for a consultation. She had been working in various capacities in the mental health field: a counselor in a residence for developmentally delayed adults, a counselor in a center for alcohol and drug rehabilitation, and similar positions at other agencies. She was very experienced and knowledgeable, but because she did not have a professional degree and license, she always hit a ceiling beyond which she could not advance. She regularly watched her peers—less skilled than her but degreed and licensed—be promoted ahead of her. She enrolled in a graduate psychology program, but found it dull and bookish, teaching things she already knew in a practical way, so she dropped out. She wondered if I might be able to help her find a way to get the more advanced and creative jobs without having to undertake the traditional schooling.

I told her I sympathized with her situation and understood how going to school felt like a huge step backwards, but that her problem was less the social order of things than her coming to terms with it. She wanted to win but didn't want to play by the rules, and thought her extraordinariness would be her excuse. She wanted to render unto God the things that she found Godlike, but dismiss Caesar. Her obstacle, I told her, wasn't the university but her attitude. If she wanted to get ahead she needed to make a commitment to ordinariness, to being ordinary. I received a letter from her a year later informing me that she had found and was well settled in a challenging graduate program. After our meeting, she said, the words "commitment to ordinariness" kept going around in her head until she realized that this was what was needed.

When we look at great people who have accomplished extraordinary feats, we see only the glamorous end results but not how they obtained them. Most of them will tell you what an ordinary, humdrum struggle it was to attain their achievement. But because the struggle was approached through the way of the small, it was experienced as a process that was not only manageable but also generated its own energy. The endeavor became less a function of the ego ("poor me, this is so hard!") and more of what Zen calls an effortless effort or an artless art. Athletes often describe this as being in the "zone."

Being ordinary, however, should never occur at the expense of being exceptional—"exceptional" here meaning excellent rather than different. We should be *ordinary but exceptional*. Jeff, a 51-year-old man, crystallized this issue in the course of therapy. An award-winning Hollywood director, he left filmmaking when the pressures overshadowed his creative process. He quickly established himself as a successful marketing consultant. Although this was better for the overall quality of his life, it wasn't challenging and he soon felt he had abandoned his creative calling. His personal life mimicked this quitting at the height of success: he had a trail of relationships with what he described as wonderful women, only to leave them just as intimacy began to lead to the possibility of marriage. He had what in Jungian psychology is called a *puer* complex, derived from the archetype of the *puer aeternus* or "eternal child." In popular psychology this is known as a Peter Pan complex (though often the misunderstanding here is that this is purely acquired rather than rooted in natural temperament). After starting a relationship with a new woman, Jeff began therapy to explore this obstacle and how to overcome it so he did not repeat this pattern.

In therapy Jeff emphasized that he wanted to get married, have children, and have a rewarding career. But whenever we delved into what this implied to him, he became ambivalent:

he didn't think he could be content in a conventional marriage because he wanted to be free to travel and creatively explore; he didn't *really* like the details of parenting, only the idea of it; and he wanted to do something creative but not in the Hollywood studio system. He often asked me what I thought he should do.

I explained that if he wanted to develop an ordinary and fulfilling life, he needed to accept his Peter Pan complex as an inherent part of himself and work through its shadowy effects—fear of intimacy and commitment. But he also needed to accept the creative and spiritual side of this complex. His assumptions of what would make him happy were largely collective: what his family and society expected from him and what he expected from himself based on this—a traditional marriage with children and a traditional role in the studio system. However, I said, there are many kinds of marriages or partnerships and many ways of being creative. Parenting is not for everyone, nor are the pressures of being in a huge organizational system. It is important to be ordinary, but ordinary doesn't necessarily mean conventional, and it definitely doesn't mean mediocre, which is what you become if you try to be ordinary in a way contrary to your nature. Instead of pushing against the things Jeff felt were wrong with his life, what would happen, I asked, if he pushed for the things that were right? He would still have to deal with his intimacy and commitment fears, but at least he wouldn't be doing so according to a script that was too large for his life.

Living small means living according to a script correctly sized to your temperament and truthful to who you are. This is what it means to be ordinary but exceptional.

KNOWING HOW TO PERSEVERE AND WHEN TO QUIT

As is the case with most of the principles for living small, a diligent, disciplined application of oneself is one's greatest asset. How you use yourself expresses your character and in turn further shapes it. The principle that perhaps most expresses and shapes character is perseverance. As the combination of patience and persistence, it is a cornerstone of the way of the small because everything else depends on it. Without it, nothing is possible. Without its element of patience, we cannot tolerate our suffering. The cause of suicide is not depression, as commonly thought, but rather, as Jungian analyst James Hillman writes, "*the urge for hasty transformation* [emphasis his]." The greater the suffering, the greater the need for patience.

Perseverance is essential when you are faced with a daunting task or are in a situation that makes you feel inept. The ability to endure may mean the difference between failure and success. Perseverance must be cultivated in small, regular doses on a daily basis. Think of George Washington: the early years of the Revolutionary War brought a series of defeats to the Americans, and the road to victory was slow and arduous. Of nine battles Washington personally led, he won only three unequivocally. He was often in retreat. The encroaching British forces and Washington's defeat at the Battle of Brandywine Creek in Pennsylvania resulted in Congress fleeing Philadelphia. But then Washington adopted a strategy of the small in his military maneuvers. This strategy, in his own words, was to "Avoid a general Action" and never "put anything at Risque." He knew that if he fought a resistance that went on long enough, persistently resuscitating itself and making slow but sure gains, he would raise the cost of victory for the British to an unacceptable level and they would eventually tire and withdraw. Though this was a defensive strategy, defined by the limitations of the Continental Army, it was aggressive and fluid. In the end, the British won most of the battles but lost the war. Ironically, two centuries later Ho Chi Minh applied a similar strategy against superior American forces in Vietnam, showing that the way of the small can work wonders and that he who is still standing at the end, stands.

Abraham Lincoln, another great master of the way of the small, also excelled in the ability to persevere. If not for this, America and probably the world would look very different today. His difficult rise to power is commonly cited: he was defeated five of the 11 times he ran for office. His perseverance during the Civil War is commendable. Like Washington, he endured terrible defeats before final victory. He was challenged personally, too. The weight of the war exacerbated the depression he was inclined toward; after losing the Battle of Fredericksburg in 1862, he exclaimed, "If there is a worse place than hell I am in it." This was less than a year after his favorite child died (he had lost another child before his presidency). And he struggled in his marriage, agonizing over his wife's sanity. Lincoln embodied the small even in victory: he encouraged a humble and forgiving attitude toward the South.

Perseverance in the face of illness or injury is just as inspiring. Whether or not actor Christopher Reeve ever had a realistic chance to stand on his own two feet was less important than the way he stood spiritually—that is, the way he stood on the strength of his character and took a stand in his life to make the most of it, struggling to accept his fate and still evolve as a person. He courageously rose to the challenge of working with limitations while not accepting false limitations. His daily routine of exercise and medical maintenance was an unsurpassable demonstration of the way of the small, especially since overlooking even the smallest detail had serious consequences. Reeve honored the small in his inner life as conscientiously as he did in his physical life. Fully inhabiting his grief, he admitted, two years after his accident, that "In the morning, I need twenty minutes to cry. To wake up and make that shift, you know, and to just say, 'This really sucks' . . . to really allow yourself the feeling of loss, even two years later . . . still needs to be acknowledged." Reeve fought his condition while embracing it, and fought until his body could no longer do so. A true warrior and Superman, he attained greatness by owning his smallness.

* * *

Most accounts of great feats of perseverance implicitly reveal two skills that must go hand-in-hand: keeping our goal, however distant, fixed in our mind, while focusing upon the step immediately in front of us. Having a clear image of our goal helps us to delay gratification and "hang in" for the duration. Focusing on what is immediately in front of us, each step and every step of the way, then helps us endure. Twelve-step programs advocate this principle when they encourage their members to take "one day at a time." Taking a deep breath, slowing down, and keeping our eyes focused in front of us is *how* we learn to persevere.

The skill of keeping a clear goal in mind furthermore enables us to not fall victim to the opposite problem of persevering too long. As the adage goes, "Genius is knowing when to quit." Because our goal is clear we can recognize when we are overshooting it. If we are at serious risk of becoming overextended or exhausted by our endeavor, we might wish to retreat, even if only for a while until it is appropriate to resume. This, the *I Ching* tells us in the hexagram "Retreat," is a sign of strength, not weakness. "We must be careful," the commentary adds, "not to miss the right moment while we are in full possession of power and position." Pushing beyond a level of saturation, beyond the point of diminishing returns, can lead to downfall. Thus did Confucius warn that "To go too far is as bad as to fall short."

Among the best examples of people who knew when to quit are the Roman ruler Cincinnatus, Washington, Truman, and Nelson Mandela. All were leaders who could have remained in their positions of power longer than they did, but they chose to be modest and small, voluntarily retiring from public life. Quitting while we're ahead can conserve our energy for other ventures. In the last decades of his life, Tolstoy curtailed his writing to pursue other interests which led to his becoming a respected sage and moral leader. In this regard, *knowing how to persevere and when to quit* are one and the same principle: they involve clearly assessing our goal and earnestly applying ourselves so that we meet the demands each step along the way, but not more than what the situation demands.

THE GREAT BEGINS WITH THE SMALL

"All beginnings are small," Jung said. This is something we often forget. Even great things have small beginnings. As Lao-tzu said,

A tree as big as a man's embrace grows from a tiny shoot.
A tower of nine stories begins with a heap of earth.
The journey of a thousand miles starts with a single step.

Dante put it this way: "A great flame follows a little spark."

Perhaps at the end of a great enterprise, we can afford to forget that all beginnings are small, but at its beginning, this could be detrimental. Probably the most dangerous pitfall of any venture is at its beginning, for we do not yet have the confidence and sustained motion to keep us going. Because beginnings attempt to create something where before there was nothing, they are especially difficult. The *I Ching* hexagram entitled "Difficulty at the Beginning" helps one navigate this with its encouraging words: "Difficulty at the beginning works supreme success." Not only do great successes often have difficult beginnings, but *it is by virtue of this difficulty and how it is worked that the great success arises.* Tour de France champion Lance Armstrong offers an illustration of this. Humiliated from finishing last in his first professional race, he nearly quit cycling altogether. His coach, upon learning how depressed he was, explained that he would learn more from this experience than from any other race in his life. He was right to have completed the race and proved to his teammates that he was a tough and reliable rider.

In the next race, Armstrong finished second, realizing he was a professional racer after all.

Quitting is not the only inappropriate way people respond to difficult beginnings. Sometimes they deal with being overwhelmed and deflated at the beginning of a venture by launching an overwhelmingly strong initiative, but this in effect can be inflated. They do more than what the situation requires, often making things more complicated or intense than they need to be and then "burning out" before reaching full stride. A number of *I Ching* hexagrams speak to this kind of imbalance, emphasizing that beginnings (and for that matter, most developments) are small and that we must therefore be accordingly small. One image the *I Ching* uses to model a proper, strong foundation for our efforts is that of a mountain. It has a sturdy, broad base—that is, it is not top-heavy or inflated—and rises gradually to the heavens. Solidly establishing and realistically pacing oneself are crucial for success.

To say that *the great begins with the small* is to say that the great is founded on the small, and that everything depends on how this foundation is laid. A difficult beginning can be a good foundation for a great ending. When adult patients suffering from the effects of childhood traumas question whether the quality of their lives can ever change, I sometimes cite the story of Winston Churchill. In spite of his birth into an aristocratic family, he had a very difficult childhood. His mother, a socialite, was self-absorbed and neglectful. He was emotionally abandoned by both parents and sent to a boarding school he detested. His pleading letters to them oozed of homesickness and a desire for parental love, but were never answered. Many biographers suspect that Churchill's depression in later life—the "black dog," as he called it—was rooted in his childhood experience. It is questionable whether Churchill would have striven to excel the way he did had he not had this legacy to egg him on. However, it is unquestionable that it contributed to his capacity to endure, a capacity which in part made him the great and timely leader he was. The moral of this story is not that difficult beginnings make great leaders (though they often do), but that a difficult beginning can help you become the person you are capable of becoming, the person you were meant to be.

The urge to become who we are capable of becoming is a natural impulse or instinct in the psyche. It is at the heart of our individuation or growth process. Our dreams are thus often concerned with new and difficult beginnings in this process and through their symbolic imagery, try to help us along. Linda, a 45-year-old single woman, had great difficulty connecting to the urge to heal herself and become who she was capable of becoming. After her entire family died while she was young, she suffered from survivor's guilt and embarked on a series of destructive relationships in which she enacted an unconscious death wish to join her family. She struggled with a tremendous sense of grief and helplessness, but even with therapy, she was unable to face her losses, to separate her fate from her family's, and to stop indulging in these relationships. One night she dreamed the following:

> I was driving on the highway. I needed to use the rest-
> room, so I pulled over at a rest stop. Before I could get
> to the door, a male dwarf appeared from nowhere, took
> his clothes off, and went into the bathroom. I followed
> and chased him out, yelling, "Get out of here, pervert!"
> The dwarf ran away.

Jungian analyst Marie-Louise von Franz observes that in fairy tales dwarves often represent creative impulses in the unconscious that have not yet emerged into consciousness. These impulses begin small but eventually prove to make all the difference in our lives. In this dream the dwarf is also a trickster—a kind of Tom Thumb figure—who provokes the dreamer to become aggressive. Through the patient's own dwarfed impulses, the dream appears to be inciting her to get active and take a creative role in her recovery process. In effect, the dream was trying to wake her up to those impulses. It is appropriate that the dwarf goes into the bathroom naked: bathroom imagery in dreams often signifies the need to expose and cleanse ourselves of psychic waste or toxic material. But Linda chases the dwarf away, which in fact was what she was doing with her own impulse to individuate, to become a ful-filled, healthy person. This dream "evidence" from her own psyche gave us the opportunity to confront this problem more directly. The dream shows not only Linda's difficulty to genu-inely begin working toward this goal, but that this beginning is naturally small—indeed, a dwarf—and naturally supported by the psyche itself.

Learn to welcome each new beginning as an exercise in nurturing the small, and remember, difficulty at the beginning of a venture is preferable to difficulty at the end.

CELEBRATING THE RIGHT DETAILS

The way of the small is very much an attention to details. This is not only because details consist of the small or intricate workings of things, but also because if you pursue an understanding of the details of any situation or phenomenon, eventually you will come to glimpse its essential nature. It is this possibility to contact the essence of things that makes the attention to details central to the way of the small. That is why Zen places such strong emphasis on cultivating an awareness of details; as the saying goes, "Zen is in the details." But we also say "God is in the details" and "The devil is in the details." Any essential ruling principle, for better or worse, finds its expression in the details. Einstein spoke about this almost poetically: "My religion consists of a humble admiration of the illimitable superior spirit who reveals himself in the slight details we are able to perceive with our frail and feeble minds."

Details are the stuff of life. I can vividly recall the moment my doctor, pointing to a fuzzy, bright spot on one of my MRI slides, said I had a brain tumor. Though shocked and frightened, I was also relieved: now I knew what was causing my symptoms. The following months of my life became an intensely focused pursuit of the small. From that moment in the doctor's office to the subsequent exploration of the options before me to the surgery itself and the following period of recuperation, my world became one of many details. Seriously studying them and seeking them out made a huge difference in the outcome. Managing them on a physical level during recovery was another matter. Indeed, Zen, God, and the devil are all in the details, and sometimes, all at once. I am alive and well today to a great extent because I paid attention to those details, as well as to the Zen, God, and devil in them. Anyone who is confronted with such a life-threatening situation needs to consider that the fine line between life and death could be just a small detail. In this position, one's eyes should be wide open, and one's appetite for details should be keen. No question is too foolish to ask, and no stone should be left unturned.

At the same time, it is important to *celebrate the right details*. It is a common human foible to focus on details and miss the big picture. We must attend to the right details. Military history once again offers some of the best examples of what can happen when the right details are celebrated, and reversely, what can happen when they are overlooked. The best warriors have always understood that, in the words of the *I Ching*,

> *[T]he superior man of devoted character*
> *Heaps up small things*
> *In order to achieve something high and great.*

How different this is from the current philosophy in vogue, "Don't sweat the small stuff." Rather, the philosophy here is, "Make the small things sweat for you."

Analyzing and taking advantage of the small things or details of given situations is what the Chinese general and military genius Sun Tzu understood as strategy. His classic treatise *The Art of War*, written around 500 BCE, is a masterpiece of both military strategy and strategies of the small. It aims to teach one how to win with a minimum of conflict: "The supreme art of war," it upholds, "is to subdue the enemy without fighting." Because its strategic way of thinking is fluid and lends itself to details of all kinds, *The Art of War* has recently been applied to fields other than military, most notably, business and management.

It has been said that Napoleon relied on *The Art of War* for his conquest of Europe. However, if this is true, he failed to apply its keen strategy at Waterloo, a terrain that his opponent, Wellington, chose and used tactically in exactly the way Sun Tzu prescribed: Wellington positioned his forces behind the back slope of a ridge that was on higher ground than Napoleon's army and sheltered from enemy fire. The small hollows of the rolling hills further concealed his troops. This is a good example of making details sweat for you.

Churchill had a most sobering experience in regard to focusing on details obvious to the eye while overlooking those in the shade. As First Lord of the Admiralty, he prepared for World War I by expanding and modernizing the British navy. He paid excruciating attention to the details of this renovation, concluding upon its completion that "Everything is ready as it has never been before. I feel sure that we shall give them a good drubbing." Not much later, Churchill's campaign in the Dardanelles and Gallipoli failed. A third of the naval force was lost and the Allies suffered over 250,000 casualties. A number of factors contributed to this. The Turkish defenses were underestimated. The Allies were not sufficiently prepared for the kind of beachhead warfare involved, this in turn giving the Turks time to rearm and reinforce themselves. The physical conditions in the trenches were terrible and the Allied soldiers suffered from disease and water and food shortages. A change of commanders midstream led to further complications. Churchill resigned shortly after and, grief-stricken, fell into a terrible depression. He would not repeat the same mistakes in his stewardship in World War II. The moral of this story was expressed by Benjamin Franklin two centuries earlier: "Watch the little things; a small leak will sink a great ship." Moreover, watch the *right* little things, for they will be the ones that go wrong.

BEING SMALL-AND-SMART

Another cornerstone principle of the way of the small is the capacity to be *small-and-smart.* It is the art of living intelligently. Smartness here does not mean cleverness in the sense of mental acrobatics or a high IQ with a lot of knowledge, but, rather, shrewdness. In the ancient mind, this was closely related to if not identical with wisdom. For instance, when Jesus said, "Be ye wise as a serpent, and gentle as a dove," he meant for us to walk in this dark world with a shrewdness or cunning equally matched to the ways of the world, yet to also walk with gentleness and peaceful intentions in our hearts.

Smartness makes smallness strong. George Washington's smart strategy compensated for the smallness of his army and resources. Other historical examples in which smallness overcame overwhelming odds include Gandhi, who shrewdly challenged the British Empire with his dual strategy of *satyagraha*, or nonviolent resistance, and shaming the British into reevaluating their policies of subjugation. Martin Luther King, Jr. borrowed much from Gandhi to battle American racial injustice through the civil rights movement. With few resources other than his character and his smarts, he changed the awareness and attitudes of millions.

On a more collective level, Japan, a nation with little land and few natural resources, rose from its ashes in the Second World War to become a leading economic power in the late twentieth century. It did this by developing a shrewd technological and manufacturing program, importing the world's raw resources to build and export high quality automobiles, motorcycles, television and audio equipment, cameras, and watches.

Israel, too, began as a small and beleaguered nation with meager resources, but with its *kibbutzim* and other ways of making the most with the least, it smartly transformed a desert into a strong agricultural and consumer economy. Israel's success was founded upon the long history of the Jews as a persecuted people living in a diaspora or exile. Few in numbers and compelled to adapt as guests in often unfriendly host nations, they had to master principles of living small in order to survive. In all these examples, perseverance was combined with smartness in the form of skill. With skill, the small can overcome great odds, as David illustrated when he defeated Goliath with a slingshot and good aim.

In the life of organizations no less than nations, small measures implemented smartly can have great results. Malcolm Gladwell, for example, describes how such measures gradually lowered the crime rate in New York City's subways in the period from 1984 to 1994. A cleaning station scrubbed off subway cars immediately after they were painted with graffiti, and fare-beaters jumping over turnstiles were arrested in full public view by police officers assigned specifically to this task. This sent a strong message that vandalism and crime would no longer be tolerated and that the subway system was being reclaimed.

Our dreams often point to the principle of being small-and-smart as well, especially when we are experiencing conflict and are inclined to overreact. A senior executive had this dream after a power shift in his corporation left him demoted while a new executive who was hostile to him took charge of the company:

> I am exploring an unknown part of my garden. There is a pond with koi fish beside my pond. It is in better shape than my pond. My wife has been secretly maintaining it. She has expended less effort to maintain it and it has clear water. My pond has muddy water.

The dreamer did in fact maintain a pond of koi fish in his garden, but his wife did not. His associations to his wife included the following: She was an accomplished, professional woman working in a politically oriented environment. She worked very hard and was successful, yet didn't get involved in organizational politics. Her nonconfrontational and charming style kept her above the fray, and she managed to get everything she needed in order to move ahead professionally. In this, the dreamer said, her orientation was different than his own. He was much more direct and confrontational. Lastly, she had strong family values, keeping her eyes on what's important.

In this dream we encounter a theme often observable in dreams when some hidden resource in the psyche becomes newly available. One finds oneself in an unknown part of one's house or office or garden. Here there is additionally a new pond with koi. That this pond is clear while the dreamer's is muddy is to say that his way of maintaining things tends to muddy the water, while his wife's way is clear and, he also confirmed, expends less energy. It is the way of the small, and it applies the principle of being small-and-smart: she is even-tempered, nonconfrontational, and focused on what's important. As the saying goes, good manners work well even with difficult people. Her charm perhaps cannot be faked by the dreamer, but the dream seems to be advising him to be more like her with regard to being shrewd, keeping a low profile, and playing his cards close to the vest. The unconscious loves puns, and it may well be that the dream is telling him that the real resource he needs to develop is the capacity to be "coy."

Literature and film, too, often point to the principle of being small-and-smart. Sherlock Holmes' career was built on this principle, and it is no coincidence that both Freud and Jung, exploring mysteries in their own right, loved detective novels.

Alfred Hitchcock was a master of the small-and-smart, if not in showing its relation to the art of living intelligently, then at least in the details that drove his stories.

A film that particularly illustrates the skill of intelligent or shrewd problem-solving is Brian De Palma's *The Untouchables*. A stylized drama of the archetypal struggle between good and evil, it pits the wily manipulation and cruelty of sociopath Al Capone (chillingly portrayed by Robert De Niro) against the youthful innocence, inexperience, and compassion of a gentle but determined Eliot Ness (smoothly played by Kevin Costner). Everything in the story hinges on the small. Ness cannot get Capone convicted on a murder charge. All he can get him for is tax evasion. His entire case against him rests on this. During the trial at the end, Ness discovers that Capone has tampered with the jury. He apprises the judge of this, but the judge sees no hard evidence for it. Intent on not letting Capone slip away one more time, Ness resorts to the kind of trickery he has learned from working on this case. Having earlier acquired Capone's payroll ledger listing Chicago officials in his patronage, he tells the judge that the judge's name is in the ledger, even though it isn't. Apparently wishing to avoid a scandal, the judge switches juries with another judge, and Capone's fate is sealed. Ness has outsmarted the judge—and Capone—with a small twist of facts. He shrewdly employed a sense of cunning surpassing even Capone's but has used it in the service of justice. Of course, this is just a movie. But its message, as with all good stories, is true to life: "Be ye wise as a serpent, and gentle as a dove."

POTENT QUOTES

*I make a song as small or as narrow as possible rather than make it
a big, broad, grand thing. By keeping it so narrow,
emotion plays a great part.*

[BOB DYLAN]

*The secret of getting ahead is getting started. The secret of getting
started is breaking your complex overwhelming tasks into small
manageable tasks, and then starting on the first one.*

[MARK TWAIN]

Everything should be made as simple as possible, but not simpler.

[ALBERT EINSTEIN]

CHAPTER FIVE

FINDING HAPPINESS

*The fountain of content must spring up in the mind, and he who hath
so little knowledge of human nature as to seek happiness by changing
anything but his own disposition, will waste his life in fruitless
efforts and multiply the grief he proposes to remove.*

[SAMUEL JOHNSON]

*It is not God's will merely that we should be happy, but that we
should make ourselves happy.*

[IMMANUEL KANT]

A SLICE OF SMALLNESS

The following recollection about the seventeenth century Japanese Zen master Bankei Yotaku has been called
"The Voice of Happiness":

> After Bankei had passed away, a blind man who lived
> near the master's temple told a friend: "Since I am
> blind, I cannot watch a person's face, so I must judge
> his character by the sound of his voice. Ordinarily

when I hear someone congratulate another upon his happiness or success, I also hear a secret tone of envy. When condolence is expressed for the misfortune of another, I hear pleasure and satisfaction, as if the one condoling were really glad there was something left to gain in his own world.

"In all my experience, however, Bankei's voice was always sincere. Whenever he expressed happiness, I heard nothing but happiness, and whenever he expressed sorrow, sorrow was all I heard."

PENETRATING WHAT IS

In both Western and Eastern mystical traditions, happiness is less about feeling good than about an attitude of acceptance of life the way it is. Happiness comes from *accepting what is, in contrast to pursuing what is not yet.* It is not dependent on anything except what is real, and really available. The philosopher Alan Watts sums up this view nicely:

The way of acceptance and spiritual freedom is found not *by* going somewhere but *in* going, and the stage where its happiness can be known is now, at this very moment, at the very place where you happen to stand. It is in accepting fully your state of soul as it is now.... The point is not to accept it *in order* that you may pass on to a "higher" state, but to accept because acceptance in itself *is* that "higher" state, if such it may be called.

Accordingly, mysticism teaches that the way to experience this higher state of acceptance is to penetrate your life *as it is given to you* and flow with it. On the one hand this involves making yourself small enough to penetrate life and let go to its flow. On the other it involves seeing life as something small and easy to penetrate and flow with, rather than an overwhelming, insurmountable obstacle.

To penetrate life means to get into it with a focused power and precision, like a laser beam. As Thoreau earlier indicated, it means "to live deep and suck out all the marrow of life." If we truly practice his favorite principle, less is more, simpler is better, we sooner or later come upon the subtler principle it reveals: *what is, is good enough*. Less is more, simpler is better works precisely because whatever exists without our inflating and overcomplicating it is good enough. Zen alludes to this principle when it says, "The beauty of a mountain is that it is so much like a mountain, and of water, that it is so much like water." The Zen poet Basho is a little more cryptic but nonetheless expresses delight in the world being exactly the way it is: "Coming along the mountain path, I am somehow mysteriously moved by these violets." Simply stated, life is simply good.

In addition to the basic goodness of life, these Zen statements underscore that life is sacred *though clothed in the profane and the common*; again, Zen is *in* the details. If we don't penetrate the profane and common—the ordinary mountain and ordinary water—we risk living only on the surface of life and missing out on its sacred dimension and beauty. Our most significant moments come from the small, focused precision with which we can penetrate life's sacredness, moments like when we are somehow mysteriously moved by violets.

Penetrating what is thus implies reaching into the heart of the present moment, where all possible satisfaction and promise for fulfillment lie. A 28-year-old single woman, Jennifer, undertook therapy, as she came to realize only later, to learn to penetrate and flow with what is. She became depressed in response to a number of converging factors, chief among which was her longstanding struggle with a weight condition. Though by no means obese, she had a large frame to begin with, and was twenty pounds heavier than she wished. She tried one diet and exercise program after another, successfully losing weight each time, only to put it back on shortly after. Even with the weight loss, she felt she was still too heavy, and the dietary and exercise regimen to keep the weight off was excruciating for her. She didn't have an eating disorder, and psychological exploration of emotional factors underlying her condition yielded no insights. Her family history had generations of heavy people.

I referred Jennifer to a physician whose clinical assessment was that her body cells were genetically predisposed to retaining fat and also, very likely, physiologically conditioned this way by early dietary and lifestyle habits. He advised against drug treatment in her case, and together they developed a dietary and exercise program that she could manage. Yet even with this, her condition continued to cause her much distress. It was her self-loathing and lack of self-compassion that made her problem so weighty. Regardless of the progress she made in therapy to understand the roots and evil effects of this self-loathing, she always returned to the fantasy position, "If only I were thin."

I concluded that if this fantasy, a form of resistance, was what Jennifer always fell back into, then this was what needed to be penetrated. We explored what she imagined her life would be like if she had a thin body. She conducted lively discussions between her "fat self" and "skinny self," and carefully probed her dreams until there came one with a wise old woman, a figure symbolizing her deeper personality or self. The woman was, perhaps to be expected, matronly and, as Jennifer described her, "pleasantly plump." Accessing and befriending this inner figure through her imagination (a process Jung called active imagination), Jennifer had many dialogues with her, both in our sessions and on her own. Such a guiding figure from the unconscious is independent from the ego, and can thus assume all the characteristics that an actual guide or teacher would in the outer world. On one occasion the woman told her that there are things about *herself* that she also didn't like but could not change. At a certain point, even wise old women just have to accept who they are and live with it—that's how they become wise. If Jennifer's weight condition was preventing her from finding fulfillment, she would never be fulfilled. Coming from within Jennifer herself, this admonition had a different effect than if it had come from me.

Over time the stigma Jennifer attached to her weight began to transform, and as she gradually made peace with her condition, she began to feel good about herself and all the good things in her life. Coincidentally, it was around this time that she met the man she eventually married. In Jennifer's instance, less is more did not mean she should lose weight. It meant that she should become small psychologically, small enough to accept her weight condition and live with it. Here, less is more, simpler is better implicitly meant what is, is good enough. For Jennifer, life would not begin "till the fat lady sang."

＊　＊　＊

The greater our suffering, the greater our need to penetrate the *meaning* it may hold for us. As Nietzsche said, "He who has a *why* to live for can bear with almost any *how*." Often the key to this meaning is small, lying in the neglected details of our life histories, the fine intricacies of our inner workings and feelings, and the subtle factors that influence our relationships. Allan, a single man in his mid-40s, poignantly illustrates this. He came to see me to deal with his depression around his condition of cirrhosis which had developed as a result of the hepatitis B virus he had contracted some time earlier from a sex partner. The hepatitis had so damaged his liver that his life had become significantly restricted, leaving him fatigued, unmotivated, and often in physical discomfort. Allan's shame about his condition and how he contracted it inhibited him from seeing friends, and his diminished social life made him very lonely. Although he was on the national wait list for a liver transplant, he discovered it could have as many complications and restrictions upon his life as the illness itself.

The early part of therapy involved an intense process of grieving. Allan grieved the loss of his health, his youth, the life he had formerly had, and the future he had hoped to have. At one point, as our discussions turned toward his childhood years, I asked him what significance this illness and dark turn of events might have from the viewpoint of his psyche, his soul. What purpose might it be serving him? This was not to suggest a psychosomatic origin for his condition or an unconscious wish or impulse to get sick. The intent was rather to place the illness into a spiritual context that is open to the mysterious significance of things *happening together,* if not in a cause-effect manner: what is it about his illness that "goes with" the rest of his life? By exploring what role the illness was having in his life story, he might discover the meaning it *could* have for him.

Allan revealed a childhood stifled by a controlling, narcissistic mother who discouraged his predisposition towards the creative arts in favor of more traditional, academic pursuits. He was made to feel very dependent on the mother, but when his younger sister was born and the mother's attentions shifted, this dependency was suddenly prohibited and shamed. He grew up emotionally isolated and often found himself shunned by schoolmates. Allan's father was a loving, gentle man, but he was under the mother's influence and unable to be an advocate for his son or to help him take a stand against the mother.

In adulthood, Allan carried this deeply internalized impression of "I-don't-count" into his relationships and career. He had few friends, and mostly short-term and unsatisfying romantic relationships. Although he found his career as a librarian in a university library modestly satisfying, it was beneath his talents and creative interests in painting, photography, and other visual arts. When he brought in samples of his work to show me, I saw he was genuinely gifted. He had abandoned his art work a few years prior to this for reasons he could not explain.

In time, by penetrating the small and painful details of his life in a small and painstaking way, slowly and carefully sifting through them, Allan connected the life-long theme of being emotionally and creatively shut down with what the cirrhosis was now doing to him. It was more of the same, but much more dramatic and life-altering. The cirrhosis was only the most recent "installment" of this experience. As he began to "own" his own role in shutting himself down, and not just blame his parents or medical condition, he saw that he had choices he could be making. He didn't have to respond to the cirrhosis the way he usually responded to diminishing experiences, which was by withdrawing and turning against himself. He opted not to pursue the liver transplant and combined a variety of treatments that arrested the growth of the cirrhosis, thereby raising the level of his physical functioning closer to what it had been before the onset of the illness. As he felt better, he began to socialize more, to risk more, and to seek a different quality of relationship than the kind to which he had been accustomed. He also began to once again enjoy doing art. Without penetrating the meaning of his illness and what his soul wanted from him, Allan might never have been compelled to change his old patterns of dissatisfaction with new ways of nourishing himself.

To penetrate what is releases the potential energy available to us below the surface of things, including the healing or reparative energy within the body and mind. Penetrating what is pierces the mysterious depths within ourselves and within the world.

KNOWING WHEN TO GO *WITH* THE FLOW AND WHEN *AGAINST*

"All things must pass," George Harrison sings. This is one of the most basic and unavoidable truths of life. Many lament over it, many avoid and live in denial of it, some accept it begrudgingly, and a few behold it as a vital facet of human existence that liberates as well as obliterates. For this beholding to be genuine, however, it must really be an act of *not* holding—that is, not trying to possess the things of life—but instead an act of letting go. In order to enjoy them, we must not clutch onto them.

The way of the small is, at heart, a surrender to life's transitory quality. Because this involves a letting-go rather than a making-something-happen, the way of the small again is, in spite of what we have said about its practical principles, an artless art, an effortless effort. The principles are basic skills, which are largely there to help us arrive at the point where we can surrender to the artless art. After all, we need to have a certain mastery over life to be comfortable enough to let go to the fact that sooner or later it sweeps away in its flow everything we dearly hold on to. We need to have what Jung described as a strong and small ego—that is, an ego that is empowered but uninflated—before we can confidently and selflessly let go of our attachments and schemes.

Not surprisingly, the fluidity of life is universally depicted in the image of water. Beginning as early as with Heraclitus, whose philosophy was encapsulated in the popular ancient saying, *panta rei* ("everything flows"), life was seen as a river whose waters are forever changing. Water is a particularly good image for the way of the small: it follows the path of least resistance; it can penetrate small places; and it is as much itself in a small cup or in small particles as it is in a huge lake. Taoism, Confucianism, and Buddhism all emulate the flowing action of water, using it as a metaphor to teach us to flow with life as it naturally unfolds rather than try to make it happen according to preconceived plans, rules, and expectations. Such fluidity involves spontaneity and a fresh response to things, and is an attitude or state of mind before it is an act. The following Zen story suggests this:

> Two monks, Tanzan and Ekido, were journeying in the mountains on their way to a neighboring monastery. At a certain point they arrived at a stream and were greeted by a beautiful young woman who was attempting to cross to the other side. She asked if they could help her, for she did not wish to get her kimono wet. Tanzan picked her up and carried her across. The mountain paths diverged and the monks silently went their way. Some hours later they came to a resting place.
>
> Ponderously, Ekido spoke: "Our order strictly forbids bodily contact with women. How is it you disobeyed the rule and picked up that woman?"
>
> Tanzan replied, "I left her back at the stream. Are you still carrying her?"

The degree to which Tanzan was strong, small, and able to let go is the degree to which Ekido was not. Tanzan's approach to life was as fluid as life itself, as the stream he crossed. This anecdote is usually referred to as a case study on the nature of attachment and detachment. However, carrying our inner and outer attachments lightly and being able to let go of them when life wants to take them from us is analogous to going with the flow.

Going with the flow will curiously bring you to what T. S. Eliot called the "still point of the turning world." This involves the experience of not moving at all and of seeing the world as not moving at all. It is the stillness of the mystic, of the Zen swordsman, of the poet who hears the voice of heaven or nature whispering into her ear. How can it be that flowing ushers in stillness? Simply put, if you go with the flow, you are *in* the flow and moving in sync with it, and therefore the flow seems to stand still. We are here not speaking of society's flow, which as Thoreau observed a century ago is like a runaway train. One has to struggle to find a way to slow down the momentum of this train as it courses through one's life and attempts to drag one away with it. In other words, there are things we should *not* flow with, for rather than bringing us to the still point of the turning world they will take us away from it. Discerning the difference between the things we should and should not flow with is not always easy.

Marjorie, a middle-aged woman who came for couple therapy with her husband, illustrates this difficulty. The problem for which they came initially appeared to be empty-nest syndrome. They were holding on to their grown daughter in a manner similar to when they were all still living together, even after the daughter had married, moved to another city, and had a baby. They cited traditional societies and lifestyles as their model for how they felt things should be. When their daughter was visiting them one week, I asked them to invite her to attend their session. Tears ran down their cheeks as they heard their daughter tell them how much she loved them, but how she needed them to get on with their lives as she had gotten on with hers. To go with the flow in this instance meant that this couple would have to appropriately change according to the natural, developmental stage of life they were at.

Immediately after this session it became evident to this couple that the problems in their own relationship that were masked by their focus on their daughter would now finally have to be dealt with. With regard to Marjorie, her sense of purpose and achievement in life was underdeveloped. An aspiring businesswoman, she had fantasies and ambitions to build a business. However, certain fears she had in pursuing these fueled her resistance to let go of her maternal role, a familiar one that could no longer be central in her life. Grieving the loss of that familiar role and working through her fears allowed her to eventually develop a business. From this she found a new wind in the second half of life.

Early in this process Marjorie had a dream in which she was swimming in the streets of her neighborhood; the streets had been transformed into canals with flowing water. She was surprised at her ability to navigate the current. This dream reflects the transformation being asked of her. The canals point to what Jung called the canalization of libido or channeling of psychic energy. Her unconscious was telling her that she needed to change the way she applied her creative life energy, to trust its flow and her ability to navigate it. She responded well to the dream's encouragement.

Later in this process, after undertaking concrete steps to start her business, Marjorie was confronted with numerous obstacles, both in the world and within herself in the form of the fears and resistance mentioned above. In our sessions she repeatedly expressed a wish to give up. At this point she had a dream which she was again able to listen to and apply. In this dream she was swimming in the same canals but upstream against a rough current. There was no danger indicated here, merely difficulty—probably the difficulty of new beginnings and of persevering. The principle portrayed here was clearly active opposition on the *ego's* part: the ego has to oppose its own inertia or inclination to go with a flow that would only keep the old status quo in place and lead to no new developments or growth. Like the salmon who needs to go against the current to return to its place of origin and give birth, we, too, must sometimes go against the flow in order to truly go with it. Life is difficult and we must battle our fears or laziness, and when others disapprove of our changes, we must battle their resistance, too. It is important to know when to go *with* the flow and when to go *against* it. Happiness is more often the fruit of hard work than the result of fortuitous things that happen to us.

The river of life is ever-changing. Owning our smallness allows us to let go in this river and then reminds us how important it is to empower ourselves to navigate it when its current gets rough or turns against us. This empowerment can come in the form of help from others, from our traditions of wisdom, or from our dreams, guiding instincts, and other inner resources. These are like oars that help steer us in the right direction and, if necessary, go against the current. Fluidity is not just going *with* the flow, as popular culture might have us believe, but a flexibility to meet life's challenges with whatever response is necessary.

SEIZING SMALL MOMENTS

The more we penetrate and flow with what is, the more present we are to seize the moment—particularly, small moments. A "small" moment is one that compresses a momentous opportunity or experience in it. Happy moments are often small moments, and sometimes, a small moment leads to great happiness—like the small doorway to heaven through which the Sufi dervishes pass. A small moment offers a special possibility of meaning, feeling, or achievement that verges on sacredness. Tennessee Williams understood this well when he said, "Sometimes there's God so quickly." Indeed, such moments are fleeting. Like shooting stars, they appear suddenly out of nowhere and are gone before we know it. They are minuscule particles in the ocean of time. They are so small that if we don't detect and seize them on the spot, we lose them forever.

Lance Armstrong gives a wonderful account of seizing a small moment which changed the course of an entire race for him. He was grouped with twenty-five other cyclists, at the front.

I could feel them wondering, *What's he thinking?*

What was I thinking? I had looked back, and saw guys were riding along, with no particular ambition. It was a hot day, and there was no incentive to pull hard, everyone was just trying to get closer to the finish line where the tactics would play out. I glanced back, and one guy was taking a sip of water. I glanced back again. Another guy was fixing his hat. So I took off. *Peoooo.* I was gone.

Armstrong writes that he rode faster than he ever had. His tactic had nothing to do with strength or ability, but depended on the initial shock and departure from the rest of the group. "I won by a minute," he explains, "and I didn't feel a moment's pain. Instead I felt something spiritual; I know that I rode with a higher purpose that day."

The art here, as Armstrong demonstrated, lies as much in the recognition of the moment as in the seizing of it. *You have to see that it is a special and rare moment.* Sometimes a small moment appears in adverse circumstances that threaten, discourage, or immobilize us. Such was the case with the violinist Itzhak Perlman in an episode told by journalist Jack Riemer. Perlman, a polio survivor who walks with leg braces and crutches, does not easily get up and down once he undoes these braces after he seats himself on the stage. During a performance in 1995 at the Lincoln Center in New York City, one of the violin strings snapped and everyone expected that Perlman would have to laboriously put his braces on again and go offstage to find another string or violin.

But he didn't. Instead, he waited a moment, closed his eyes and then signaled the conductor to begin again.

The orchestra began, and he played from where he had left off. And he played with such passion and such power and such purity as they had never heard before. Of course, anyone knows that it is impossible to play a symphonic work with just three strings. I know that and you know that, but that night Itzhak Perlman refused to know that. You could see him modulating, changing, recomposing the piece in his head. At one point, it sounded like he was de-tuning the strings to get new sounds from them that they had never made before.

When he finished, there was an awed silence in the room. And then people rose and cheered. There was an extraordinary outburst of applause from every corner of the auditorium. We were all on our feet, screaming and cheering, doing everything we could to show how much we appreciated what he had done.

He smiled, wiped the sweat from his brow, raised his bow to quiet us and then he said—not boastfully, but in a quiet, pensive, reverent tone, "You know, sometimes it is the artist's task to find out how much music you can still make with what you have left." What a powerful line that is. It has stayed in my mind ever since I heard it.

As we could see, improvisation of this sort is very much the art of seizing small moments. The small moment wasn't just when the violin string snapped, but when Perlman "waited a moment, closed his eyes and then signaled the conductor to begin again." In the moment that he took to compose himself and pensively penetrate the situation, he decided to flow with it. This capacity had probably been cultivated from long years of discipline as a violinist. Disciplines like cycling and playing an instrument inherently *are* the way of the small, for they demand not only perseverance and attention to details, but penetration and fluidity. Above all, Perlman honored the small in this regard: in humbly accepting the task "to find out how much music you can still make with what you have left," he sided with his *own* smallness and turned an otherwise ordinary and even banal moment into a sacred one.

Sadly, we sometimes miss such promising moments because we do not recognize them until too late. I can recall the grief I experienced one time when I missed a small, divine moment that could have been shared with Jackie, a patient whom I had been treating for about four years and with whom I had developed a warm, intimate relationship. One session, as we were saying goodbye at the end of our hour, I felt an impulse to hug her. I wondered what this urge was, but before I could even fully register it in my consciousness she was out the door. When it did register, I realized it was a feeling of gratitude and love—gratitude for having had the opportunity to work with her, and love for who she was. "Oh well," I figured, "there will be another time."

Four days later I received a phone call informing me that Jackie had collapsed and died from a massive heart attack. Naturally, I was shocked. She was 60. I realized that my intuition to hug her may have been my unconscious mind's way of telling me to say goodbye to her.

In the period ahead, as I grieved the loss of Jackie, using our appointment time to read over my notes from our sessions and her dreams, poems, and other writings, I also grieved the loss of that sudden, ethereal moment I never seized. How many times I wished that I had acted upon it, showing her how much I appreciated her and our work together. I had to admit to myself that I had had a sneaking feeling *in that moment* that something was awry, and that deep down I knew I was keeping this strange urge at arm's length rather than reaching for it. Getting caught in the role of therapist, instead of just grabbing and running with it, I decided to wait to "fully register it in my consciousness"—meaning, I had to intellectually understand it. To have flowed around this, I would have had to let go of that role the same way Tanzan let go of his role as a monk with the lady at the stream or Perlman let go of the conventional idea of playing a violin with four strings. I would have had to tolerate the insecurity of not understanding—or what in Zen is called "don't-know-mind"—and I would have had to tolerate the emotional vulnerability of reaching out purely on an impulse. All this points again to the importance of having an ego that is as small and as strong as possible—small enough to fit into such brief moments, and strong enough to take the risk to let go and flow. To seize small moments, we ourselves need to be small so as to get out of our own way.

Mysteriously, my experience had what felt like a redeeming conclusion, which most small moments that are lost regrettably do not. On the eve of the Thanksgiving that came not long after Jackie's death, she appeared in a dream and gave me a big, warm hug. No words were exchanged. Seeing her filled me with joy. Everything I would have wanted to say to her was implicitly understood. The dream had a numinous, otherworldly quality, and for me it was a very special thanksgiving.

LETTING GO OF PERFECTION

Striving for perfection is often confused with the quest for fulfillment: we think that if we can become perfect or create perfect things or situations, we will be happy. This is a form of grandiosity, and not the way of the small.

There are various theories of perfectionism, ranging from psychology, genetics, and biochemistry to astrology. But regardless of its origins, few can dismiss its essential flaw: in the final analysis, nothing is perfect. Perfection is an ideal, not a fact. As a patient I treated once said, perfection is a good goal, as long as it remains just that—a goal. If it becomes a reality, it becomes too limiting.

Perfectionism occurs as a compensation for our smallness—as an effort to correct or fix it—when we judge our smallness as inferior, inadequate, or "less than." In this, it is similar to other forms of grandiosity, such as conceit and arrogance—indeed, the belief that we can be perfect or create perfection is itself a conceit and an arrogance. However, perfectionism has one striking difference from other forms of grandiosity: it can disguise itself as the way of the small because it is so focused on details and getting them right. In fact, though, perfectionism is the celebration of details beyond limits. It is too much of a good thing. Pushed to an extreme, it can become a disease, taking over our work, our appreciation of material objects, and our personal relationships. The search for a perfect partner and the intolerance of the flaws and mistakes of others are common traits of the perfectionist. Perfectionism here is especially deadly, for objects can be made to simulate the perfect, but people can't. Jungian analyst Donald Kalsched calls the mind, when it becomes too critical, a tyrannical perfectionist. This behavior, he explains, is a defense not only against connection with others, but with our own innate capacities for love and other positive qualities; we are never good enough. Again, perfectionism is an unconscious compensation for our own imperfection and smallness, or rather, our inability to accept and tolerate these.

Perfectionism is also unconscious spirituality. It is idealism unintegrated into real life. As such, it is both a spiritual and emotional tyranny. Religious training in every tradition warns against the godlike aspiration to be perfect, for it breeds hubris. I remember visiting an esteemed master of Zen and the art of pottery in Japan. As he saw me fumbling hopelessly while trying to make a tea bowl in his class, he showed me how to do it. With his hands he made a clay bowl whose circular shape and internal hollow were so perfect I was dumbstruck. Only a machine could have done that, I thought. After completing it, he put a slightly damaging indentation into the side of the bowl. When I asked his interpreter why he did that, she said, "Perfection is only for the gods, and not natural for this world." And of course, if that's the case, one would not wish to tempt the gods.

Here we come to the question that if perfection were truly divine, wouldn't it be permitted to be part of the natural scheme of things? Is God so removed from this world that perfection can only exist on his side and not ours? Stated reversely, is imperfection a part of the natural scheme of things for a special, divine purpose, fulfilling some attribute of God himself? Perhaps the mark of imperfection the Zen potter made on the side of the bowl *was* a sign of God. Perhaps imperfection and mistakes are part of the big picture, rooted not only in our personal nature but also in the transpersonal as part of God's design and way of manifesting in the world. To suffer imperfection and mistakes in matters of love and in our work, or with the small and great moments we miss, is not only unavoidable, but integral to the spiritual fabric of life. Without imperfection and suffering, there can be no transformation. Jungian analyst Edward Edinger has put his finger on why it is important to understand this principle:

> It is the almost universal mistake of the ego to assume total personal responsibility for its sufferings and failures. We find it, for instance, in the general attitude people have toward their own weaknesses, an attitude of shame or denial. If one is weak in some respect, as everyone is, and at the same time considers it ignominious to be weak, he is to that extent deprived of self-realization. However, to recognize experiences of weakness and failure as manifestations of the suffering god striving for incarnation gives one a very different viewpoint.

The "suffering god striving for incarnation" is the quintessential Christian vision of God. Its premise is that by incarnating as a man into the world of man, God takes on our imperfection and suffering as part of *his* completeness. By becoming human and all that it implies, he becomes a fuller God.

The Jewish vision of God, by contrast, assumes that God does not have to take on imperfection because he is not perfect to begin with. God himself indicates this in the Book of Genesis when he reveals his sense of failure and disappointment with the fallible creature he has made, namely, man. (First comes the expulsion from the Garden of Eden and then the Flood, but the Hebrew Bible offers other examples, too, of God's limitations.) Though not in explicitly theological language, a Jewish story illustrates the "very different viewpoint" one gets when imperfection is recognized as a manifestation and instrument of the divine:

> There once was a king in times of old. One day he acquired a beautiful, huge diamond, the largest and most beautiful he had ever seen. He kept it wrapped in a special box and had it guarded. Every day he took it out to admire it, as he loved it very much.
>
> One day he accidentally dropped the diamond and a scratch marred its surface. The king became very upset. He called together the finest jewelers in his kingdom to see what they could do to remove the scratch. They deliberated among themselves as to what could be done. They took the diamond away and returned it a day later

after polishing the surface, but this made the scratch even more noticeable.

The king was even more upset. He offered a reward to anyone in the kingdom who could restore the diamond to its original beauty. A man appeared and said, "Give me the diamond for a day, and I will try my best." The king agreed.

The next day the man returned with the diamond. The king unwrapped it, and to his amazement he saw that the man had carved a beautiful rose into the diamond, using the scratch as the stem. Now it was truly the most magnificent diamond in the world, and the king was as happy as he could be.

The way of the small is beyond perfection because it is purposely less than perfect. It aims to embrace imperfection as an expression of the fullness, beauty, and divine nature of things. To drink of these, we must *let go of perfection*.

LEARNING TO LOVE VULNERABLY

After all that has been written about it—in the Bible and other great scriptures of the world, by Shakespeare and the poets and philosophers—love still remains a profound mystery. Yet one cannot doubt that this unfathomable source of happiness has something to do with the way of the small.

Perhaps the strongest indication that love *is* the way of the small is that this is the only way we can love. We can never love so completely that we exhaust love's possibilities and its capacity to surprise us. It is an ocean one can never finally cross, and thus, the fullness it brings lies in our realization of how small we are in it and how fully it can surround us. Furthermore, love is the way of the small because one can only love by being small and humble. As St. Paul said, "Love is patient and kind; love is not jealous or boastful; it is not arrogant or rude. Love does not insist on its own way." And then there's the fact that, given its oceanic depth and breadth, we can only drink it in small doses. Yes, there do occur experiences in which we get swept away by its awesome might, but by and large, love is a gentle, slow affair—one day at a time, one gesture at a time.

Love is not a feeling, as so many people think. You do not have to *feel* love in order to love. Indeed, often the greatest, most courageous acts of love are born when we feel love least. And yet, we know love most immediately, most transparently, when we feel it. If feelings are not love itself, they do announce its presence. We can infer much about love from what James Hillman writes about feeling:

> Perhaps, feeling can be defined as the art of the small—the shade of difference, the subtle emphasis, the little touch. It can watch a relationship unfold, gardening it along, husbanding the forces.

And:

> Personal relationships require personal feeling. Here, the emphasis is on the small. The mystics can instruct

us. We like to believe that the great mystics occupy themselves with the vaster cosmic things, but they usually talk about small things, very small things. With the feeling function they reduce intellectual speculation to matters close at hand, personal issues of food and nature. Their laughter is born from trivia. Our spoiled feelings are usually resentments over small things, those little mistakes that have been neglected as one goes along. Then life turns sour: one has soured one's life by missing the small feeling opportunities and one is left with festering minor irritations. To miss the small is to miss with one's feeling function. Therefore, personal feeling needs to be expressed in small ways: personal favors, personal sharing, personal remarks about exactly what one likes in the other. The feeling function, by recognizing the other person's virtues, connects him to these parts, giving him belief in himself. Personal feeling is also expressed in small ways with *eyes*, *voice*, and *hands*.

Simply stated, to attend to what we feel in small ways is to serve love.

If love is beyond measure in its depth and breadth, it is small in its vulnerability. Like many living organisms, it is delicate, and like any living organism, it needs to be nurtured. If it is not, it spoils, or worse, never blooms. We see this all the time in episodes of dissociated love, with people who do not realize how much they love someone until he or she dies, or when they simply love someone and can't express it. The film *The Remains of the Day* richly captures the charged but repressed love between the protagonists played by Anthony Hopkins and Emma Thompson. Unable to act upon their deep feelings for each other, it is a tragic story of failed love. Divorce, too, whether it has to do with people's incompatibility, different directions of growth, wandering hearts, or a gradual deadening is the hammer blow of failed love. That this can happen with something that initially *felt* like it was invulnerable and eternal comes as a rude awakening to most of us. Hermann Hesse poignantly writes:

> *How heavy the days are.*
> *There's not a fire that can warm me,*
> *Not a sun to laugh with me,*
> *Everything cold and merciless,*
> *And even the beloved, clear*
> *Stars look desolately down,*
> *Since I learned in my heart that*
> *Love can die.*

This vulnerability of love, this tenderness, is characteristic not only of the love between lovers, but the *eros* or passion one has for *anything*, be it an idea or ideal (such as beauty), or a creative vision or calling (such as one's art or profession). If not nurtured, it fails to flourish. The same is true with other kinds of love as well, including *philia* (brotherly love or friendship), *storge* (parental love for one's child), and *agape* or *caritas* (altruistic love or compassion for all people and also the love of God). And, not to be forgotten, our love for ourselves is important, too. I am here referring not to narcissistic excess, but a healthy self-valuing that in turn allows us to love and be loved by others. Jesus presumed we have such self-love when he said, "love thy neighbor as thyself." Self-love is also compassion for ourselves. If compassion is, as someone once said, standing with another in their diminishment, then it must naturally include accepting ourselves in our own diminishment. Too often we react to our feeling small with shame or self-contempt. All love that opens itself to the depths of the soul, whether in ourselves or others, purposely sides with the vulnerability and tenderness of the soul. Itself vulnerable and tender, this love must be carefully protected and watered with *acts* of love that express and help it grow. Without this, it can dry up. Although mysteriously divine, it is also all too human.

This said, love holds together many opposites, and can be tough as well as tender. Hollywood has made an industry from stories about love that endures the worst imaginable hardships. However, it is the notion of "tough love" as it has recently come to be known in the self-help movement that speaks directly to the way of the small. In asserting that even love is subject to limits, tough love harks back to the teachings of St. Thomas Aquinas and the Talmud, namely, that a love that is misdirected or unbalanced can be harmful to others, not to mention ourselves. In our modern culture of narcissism, in which self-centeredness runs rampant, it is important to recognize that saying "No" to people is sometimes the best way to love them. A child who is misbehaving or a spouse with a gambling or drinking problem needs us to say "No" to them if they cannot say "No" themselves.

For many, refusing others is a hard lesson to learn, bringing up such feelings as guilt and fear. This is a matter that requires us to live in our skin—that is, close to our instincts—in contrast to living in *other* people's skin. Codependency, for which tough love is the best medicine, is a commingling of instincts. One supports or takes on responsibility for someone else's instinctual indulgences as if they were one's own. It is arguable whether this is love at all, much less misdirected or unbalanced love. Living in our skin in such instances means saying "No" to our *own* tendencies to accomodate the excesses of others and being comfortable enough with ourselves to then say "No" to them. Like tough love, this is another application of less is more, simpler is better.

Possibly the way that love most vividly evokes the way of the small is with the vulnerability it brings up in us. Love opens us to the depths of the soul. It exposes us not only to all that is worthy of love in ourselves and each other, but also all that is unworthy (or at least all that we feel and believe is unworthy). Love is intimately related with our shadow, our dark side. The shadow consists of our undesirable qualities—our neediness, weaknesses, ugly traits, our wounded, "sick stuff." These qualities are all part of who we are and require our acceptance as much as our more positive features. A dream I had during a difficult period hinted at the connection between love and the shadow, and the importance of being vulnerable or open to it. There were no events or images, merely a voice that woke me from my sleep when it said,

"Love is a sickness relived/relieved." The words "relived" and "relieved" were somehow said at the same time as one word, as if to suggest they were the same thing. This occurred in the magical way things happen in dreams. The effect, though, was anything but magical. It brought a sobering realization that love forces us to relive old wounds, and it is in reliving and working them through that we may find relief and redemption. Love can be not only joyful, but painful; not only a heaven, but a hell.

The way of the small must then step in to also help us prevent ourselves from falling back upon our defenses against the vulnerability that love brings up in us. There are a variety of defenses available to us for this purpose—denial and avoidance, projection, even sabotaging love. One of the most common and insidious ways we protect ourselves is the abuse of power. Feeling vulnerable and powerless, we resort to controlling the other as a way to mask and divert attention from this. "I want you to do it my way," or "I'm right!" is how this dynamic unfolds. But it never works, for the controls we put on a situation to avoid exposing our vulnerability either fail to hold up or altogether stifle and kill love. This is why St. Paul said, "Love does not insist on its own way." This doesn't mean we shouldn't fight in a relationship for what we believe. Rather, we should not fight at the expense of our vulnerability, for if we do, we fall right into the grip of the worst elements of our shadow. Then, instead of consciously *having* or *owning* our shadow as part of who we are, we are unconsciously had or owned by *it*, and divided not only against the other, but ourselves.

The power of love is inversely proportional to the love of power. Within a relationship the more we relinquish our desire to be in a powerful position over the other, the more we can experience genuine love. The power of love is the power or strength to be vulnerable. To be vulnerable is to be small, and to be small is to be vulnerable. There are many ways of loving. One may love from a distance, one may love stoically, one may love possessively, one may love by showering the other with attention. Loving vulnerably is the kind that is most intimate, for it shares the deeper parts of ourselves and invites the other into our inner sanctuary.

FACING ADVERSITY WITH HUMOR

No discussion of happiness would be complete without some mention of humor. Particularly for the way we are here conceiving happiness—as the acceptance of one's life as it is given to one—humor is vital. Humor helps us to flow with life, to deal with its hardships and setbacks. The ability to see the humor in things puts them into perspective, keeping them small when necessary and keeping us small when we take ourselves too seriously. In Latin, *humor* means "moisture" and "fluid," and is connected with *umere*, "to be moist" or "moisten." We may say that humor moistens the dryness of life and restores its fluidity.

Humor is essential to psychotherapy. In cases of depression, it helps patients digest what is happening to them. In daily life, humor helps us to accept and live with our diminishment, loss, and suffering. It is no accident that Jews, a people with a long history of persecution, oppression, and slaughter, are famous for their humor. A Holocaust survivor recalls the following about coping with life in the camps:

> There was a lot of humor about ourselves, about what we do . . . . We made a joke out of every situation, we made fun, yes, why not, how can you live any other way? Look, if I say I'll die, I'll die. You'll die before you're dead. You should know there were many people who died before their time was up because they did not know how to laugh at themselves. We had to!

No doubt, the humor in the camps—gallows humor—was dark, but it appropriately matched the circumstances. Freud said that in fact there are no jokes, only circumstances condensed and veiled in humor. But any way you turn it, humor helps you remain human in intolerable or painful situations. The challenge here is to *face adversity with humor*, to keep your humor when everything is conspiring against it. The question this then raises is, what makes it possible for us to find humor in such situations? Many peoples have suffered cruelties similar to the kind inflicted on the Jews, but never developed a sense of humor about them. As Murray Horowitz of National Public Radio said, "There's not a lot of Armenian comedians."

Certainly, one factor that oils the wheel of humor is the ability to laugh at ourselves, an ability we acquire only when we have an attitude of smallness about ourselves and our significance in the cosmos. We must be able to laugh not only at our circumstances but also at our flaws and foibles. Our smallness both makes humor possible and in turn is healthily reinforced by humor. Again the Jews, a people who survived by learning to be strong while small, demonstrate their self-confidence by their ability to mock themselves and their predicament. Let us conclude this chapter with a joke that illustrates this:

> Two elderly Jewish men, Moishe and Chaim, are sitting on a park bench reading newspapers. Moishe is reading the *Jerusalem Post*. Chaim is reading a fervently anti-Semitic weekly published by a neo-Nazi group. Seeing this, Moishe turns to Chaim and says, "Chaim, how can you read that rag? All it has in it is hatred for the Jews."
>
> Chaim responds: "You know, Moishe, I used to read what you're reading, but it was always filled with bad news about the problems of Israel and of Jews everywhere. I like this paper better. It says the Jews run the government, the Jews are all millionaires, the Jews run the newspapers and television networks, the Jews own all the big companies and run Wall Street, the Jews run the big universities. This is good news!"

POTENT QUOTES

Ring the bells that still can ring.
Forget your perfect offering.
There is a crack in everything.
That's how the light gets in.

[LEONARD COHEN]

We can do no great things, only small things with great love.

[MOTHER TERESA]

Blessed are we who can laugh at ourselves,
for we shall never cease to be amused.

[PROVERB]

CHAPTER SIX

EMBRACING DIMINISHMENT

*When you think that you've lost everything, you find out
you can always lose a little more.*

[BOB DYLAN]

The experience of the self is always a defeat for the ego.

[C.G. JUNG]

A SLICE OF SMALLNESS

The following was written by a young man shortly after his
art exhibit was vandalized and plundered. Listen to the
soul's grief, and grief's soul:

> The intense feelings of sorrow yesterday, the night
> beginning at dusk when I tried to sleep, the night of
> disbelief at what people will do. The bronze sculp-
> ture gone, the black painting torn. My pot broken,
> sand spilled, the terrible chattering room—the death
> of my life. At first I could not utter a sound, then
> it was hopeless to do so. Just a pot. Just a sculpture.

Just a painting. Just a life and a life—my life. They
say build another pot, make another sculpture, but
they do not realize that life in each has its distinct
essence never to be in another form. Where does the
spirit of such life go? Why are people so cruel and
thoughtless of life? I can build, and will new life,
but I am so painfully ashamed at the awareness of
people. Art should never be locked or guarded from
the lives of people. Why can they not be as noble as
the breath given them? What is art to be guarded,
locked, policed, untouched?

Why can man not realize that his life and that of all
life are the same and that each has its identity only in
the ability to share essences? This incident is a haunting reminder of the weak morality of our *well* society.
They feed on the waste of their own existences and
think it alive and beautiful.

I learned pain this day. I learned pain. We never
own our lives or anything. Our possession is *nothing*.
Naked of want, nothing remains! We do not really create anything. We are but the means to present another
individual entity without claim to its life. At any time
the pot can be broken. Broken! Broken! Broken! The
trees make no lament, yet they know the same awaits
them. And we also know. Why are men so insensitive
to beauty? I cannot stand their coarse screams and the
murder of whatever God means in Beauty. Where is
nowhere where one can be at peace?

This experience has taught me much pain. We can not be so foolish as to be possessors of life. We can not be so vain as to say "ours." We do not create anything by cognitive wish, only by the love felt of the material, but then we must guard against the desire to hold. How hard it is to be content with the empty left by something we love that has gone.

Someone must have had a great need to possess my sculpture to have taken it. But gladly would I have given it to anyone who would have loved it. This does not trouble me nearly so much as the death of my pot. To be a destroyer of life is immorality. . . . The life of these words to you is perhaps my new beginning.

The swallow always wins, even now I feel better and maybe I will be able to work again. I hope so. To meet the matter death with calm is the only way, perhaps, to life.

SURRENDERING TO THE INNER DESERT

The way of the small is not only something we voluntarily choose when it suits us. It is a principle of life that may also impose itself upon us whether we ask for it or not, coming upon us as a matter of fate, personal fate. In this, it can diminish us in ways we do not like, beyond what we might ordinarily find acceptable, and often, it does so with no known reason or rationale. We are *made* small, and if we should be resistant to this, as could be expected, then the way of the small goes to work on that, eating up our resistance through our failed efforts to escape this fate. Perhaps then we reach a place of desperation, alone and abandoned—abandoned by the world, by life, even by God himself, or so it seems. Then we find out if we truly live the way of the small, for the only thing that can now be left to us is our *furthering* the way of the small by surrendering to it and giving it free reign, helping it along by our active self-diminishment. This is no longer an act of depression or desperation, for if we have really bottomed out, these, too, have been diminished and consumed. Now we are in new, unknown territory.

St. John of the Cross calls this experience of diminishment the "dark night of the soul," and explores its nooks and crannies in his classic works, *The Ascent of Mount Carmel* and *The Dark Night*. The alchemists understood it as *mortificatio*, or inner death. Zen refers to it as the "great doubt," portraying its stages in the famous Oxherding Pictures and its disorienting effects in numerous anecdotes. Moses, the Prophets, Jesus, and the fourth-century Desert Fathers underwent this emptying-out of attachments through their desert wandering. Jonah had his own variation in the belly of the whale. And of course, who could forget Job? In the hands of Satan and with God's collusion, he was reduced to utter smallness and despair. Dante's descent into hell itself begins as a midlife crisis when he finds himself lost in the "dark wood" at the outset of *The Divine Comedy*. Finally, in his autobiography Tolstoy vividly describes the living hell he fell into when he discovered how meaningless his life had become after years of success as a writer and a Russian count: nearly committing suicide, it took several more years for him to traverse his desert of darkness.

The hallmark of such profound diminishment is its destruction of our dearly held assumptions of how things work: what supported or nourished us before no longer does. This can come in response to some radical event in our lives—the loss of a loved one, the death of a dream, a business failure, an accident, a health crisis—or it can just come imperceptibly out of nowhere, out of the unconscious. Crossing over into the second half of life—the midlife transition—can trigger it, too, as there begins the steady decline toward old age and all that this brings. A natural loss occurs as we watch our energies and capacities slowly decrease. Our unfulfilled hopes must now be squarely faced and grieved, this deepening our sense of loss. Whatever the case, it is as if life's various forms of diminishment are but preparations for the ultimate diminishment we must sooner or later face—death. Death is the absolute minimalist, taking away our very lives and all that we cherish. The way of the small is a way of life *and* death, since the two inevitably go together.

According to most mystical traditions, the purpose of a diminishment experience is to raze down the ego to the source that gives it its true strength. Mysticism attempts to provide a framework for this. It normalizes this experience—as crazed as we may become from it—by showing us that it is a natural part of life. The desert must be endured—in the case of Moses and the Israelites, for forty years, in the case of Jesus, for forty days (40 symbolizes a complete period). Only then can the transformation occur that comes from suffering the desert. In the Hebrew Bible this transformation is expressed in the image of the promised land. In the New Testament it is conveyed through Jesus' resurrection and ascension to heaven; the crucifixion was the ultimate diminishment that capped his desert wandering. Mystics have always understood these events as inner experiences that everyone can have, and not only as episodes of religious history.

By normalizing our diminishment, mysticism also *advances* it. It understands that diminishment, once accepted, potentially leads to transformation. This is not a trick designed to get us out of diminishment or convert it into something positive, for the suffering of life does not disappear simply because we have accepted it. In fact, the desert may be an inner place we visit again and again as a prerequisite to spiritual renewal. Edward Edinger explains how this recurring process creates the cyclic, spiraling course of psychological growth: The ego gets too big or comfortable for its own good, leading to some experience of wounding or diminishment. This then is transformed by an attitude of surrender or sacrifice, resulting in a humble acceptance of the new condition. And finally, the process repeats, but hopefully on a more evolved level. Diminishment is thus a vital part of the life process, offering its own special route to fulfillment. As the ego becomes smaller and smaller, the inner self—the kingdom of God within—is realized.

How, you might ask, can the kingdom of God be realized in a situation of diminishment, in a condition of deprivation and woundedness? Is this not contrary to all the wonderful and delightful things we associate with the kingdom of God or religious experience? The Trappist monk Thomas Merton sets this matter straight:

> It is in this darkness, when there is nothing left in us that can please or comfort our own minds, when we seem to be useless and worthy of all contempt, when we seem to have failed, when we seem to be destroyed and devoured, it is then that the deep and secret selfishness that is too close for us to identify is stripped away from our souls. It is in this darkness that we find true liberty. It is in this abandonment that we are made strong. This is the night which empties us and makes us pure.

Thoreau, too, understood the paradox of this dark night of the soul, this desert that dries out the ego's inflation and attachments. "Not until we are lost," he said, "do we begin to understand ourselves." This kind of religious experience is known in Western mysticism as the *via negativa*, or path of negation. The Hindu mystics refer to it as *neti, neti*—"not this, not that"—and Buddhism's Nagarjuna described it with his fourfold negation that concludes that nothing descriptive can be said about nirvana. Such a religious experience diminishes the ego by deflating its self-importance and certitude, thus making it small enough to encounter the divine in its pristine, naked form. The premise here is that God and his kingdom prefer to be *small*, and are empty and selfless. Not just blinding light, but impoverishing darkness. The kingdom does not emerge *out of* our diminishment. It is found *in* our diminishment.

If you should find yourself in the inner desert, *surrender* to it.

SACRIFICING YOURSELF TO THE JAWS OF DEFEAT

When we discussed in an earlier chapter the tragic experience of Christopher Reeve, we touched upon the depth of his despair. But we were hardly able to get a real sense of what he must have gone through in his ordeal of coming to terms with his loss. Can anyone who has not undergone such an ordeal imagine what it must be like to go horseback-riding one day at the pinnacle of one's life and wake up five days later paralyzed from the shoulders down? Diminishment of this kind seems impossible to accept. While most people will never have to face this kind of diminishment, many of us will probably have to face, at one time or another, an experience of inner paralysis, an experience in which we have been shut down or cut down in our morale and wherewithal. In this, our faith and hope become diminished along with our capacities to do anything about it. From the hard-earned wisdom of their ordeals, people like Christopher Reeve can teach us much about how to cope with such experiences.

One of the principles of the way of the small often evident in the recollections of such people is self-sacrifice. It takes surrender one step further—one not only gives up, but gives *oneself* up. The deeper the diminishment, the deeper the sacrifice that is demanded from us. As Abraham knew from his episode with Isaac, and then Jesus from his ordeal, this sacrifice can be all-consuming. As long as there still remains an "I" or an ego that is separate from the sacrifice, it is not complete. This of course does mean to literally sacrifice our lives. As Reeve bravely concluded, death is an easy way out compared to *living* with the diminishment and sacrifice. The *real* sacrifice is to *embrace* the diminishment rather than try to get out of or minimize it. Though efforts to escape it are perfectly human, they usually fail because the diminishment is so overwhelming. Furthermore, they set us up in opposition to the diminishment, going against the way of the small rather than with it. This is not to suggest that we should make our diminishment worse than it is—that's martyrdom or masochism, not sacrifice. Rather, it is to say that we should move *toward* our diminishment, not *away* from it. This is the most spiritual form of less is more.

Thus the principle of sacrifice—the bravest form of embracing diminishment—implies *putting ourselves voluntarily into the jaws of defeat*, or at least submitting ourselves to them once they have snared us in their teeth. Naturally, this feels counterinstinctive, but in fact it is not. It is driven by an instinct of the higher or inner self, which in demanding our self-sacrifice goes against our lower, more primitive self-preservation instincts. The conflict between these two types of instinct makes the task of sacrifice *feel* counterinstinctive, but this feeling, disturbing as it is, is just a side effect of that conflict. It is to be anticipated from any task that is an *opus contra naturam*, or a "work against nature." This is the term the alchemists used to describe their efforts to free the soul from its material and natural view of itself and the world.

Listen to how the following figures champion their personal defeat in this work that goes against nature but serves their higher nature. The poet Rainer Maria Rilke:

What is extraordinary and eternal
does not want to be bent by us.
I mean the Angel who appeared
to the wrestlers of the Old Testament . . .
Whoever was beaten by this Angel
(who often simply declined the fight)
went away proud and strengthened
and great from that harsh hand,
that kneaded him as if to change his shape.
Winning does not tempt that man.
This is how he grows: by being defeated, decisively,
by constantly greater beings.

And the existential psychologist Clark Moustakas:

> The lonely sufferer helps himself to a fuller realization of self, not by reducing his sense of pain and isolation, but by bringing its full extent and magnitude to consciousness. Great loneliness and suffering are met creatively, as potential growth experiences, only by surrendering to them, fully and completely. Salvation, self-growth, lies in giving full assent to loneliness and suffering, accepting what is, not fighting or resisting, not rationalizing or appealing to external helps, not demanding to know why one has been singled out for so much pain, but submitting one's self to the experience in total self-surrender.

We see in these authors a commitment, and moreover, a yearning, to inhabit their diminishment as fully possible. It is as if they are saying: "What *more* has life taken from me? Let me go there and inhabit *that*. Let me be less even more." If embracing diminishment in this way does not end suffering or convert it into something positive, it also does not preclude the joy of victory that we snatch from the jaws of defeat by placing ourselves into them and purposefully living small. This is not the joy and victory of a heroic ego touting its conquest, but the spiritual joy and victory of the inner self. Again Thomas Merton writes:

> Do not look for rest in any pleasure, because you were not created for pleasure: you were created for spiritual JOY. And if you do not know the difference between pleasure and spiritual joy you have not yet begun to live.
>
> Life in this world is full of pain. But pain, which is the contrary of pleasure, is not necessarily the contrary of happiness or of joy. . . . Pleasure, which is self-ish, suffers from everything that deprives us of some good we want to savor for our own sakes. But unselfish joy suffers from nothing but selfishness. Pleasure is re-strained and killed by pain and suffering. Spiritual joy ignores suffering or laughs at it or even exploits it to purify itself of its greatest obstacle, selfishness.

This is how diminishment can play a vital part in happiness. It offers an opportunity to free happiness from the shackles of suffering, if not the suffering itself. Indeed, as Merton indi-cates, suffering and happiness, pain and joy, are not mutually exclusive: they can coexist, and perhaps the tolerance of suffering is the greatest possible test for the depth of our happiness. It is the *shackles* of suffering—the attachment to pleasure and to ourselves, the investment to escape from suffering—that inhibit happiness. To free ourselves from these, we must be willing to sacrifice ourselves to the jaws of defeat. But it is not only freedom and a happiness rooted in freedom that are won by this sacrifice. To "sacrifice," as the word and act were originally understood, means to consecrate, to make sacred. By sacrificing ourselves to the jaws of defeat, we consecrate ourselves and make our suffering sacred.

The importance of this cannot be overestimated. Patients in psychotherapy often struggle with their suffering. Sometimes they feel it is more than they can bear. In many instances, I ask them if they can make their suffering sacred. Can they perhaps create something from their suffering—a poem or piece of contemplative writing, a painting, sculpture, or photograph, or a ritual acknowledgment of some kind? Can they ask their suffering what it "wants" from them or what it "wants" to teach them, and to try to somehow express this creatively? This is a way to engage their suffering in a direct and deep way, making it sacred. It not only helps patients to weather their suffering, but to fathom the meaning it may have for them. And very significantly, it helps them to honor it as a potentially beautiful if also ugly experience (paradoxical as this may again sound). After all, much of the world's great art has come from people who turned their anguish into something beautiful. At least in some measure, suffering is redeemed by the wisdom and beauty to which it gives birth. One may think of the story told by the young artist at the beginning of this chapter or the poem by Rilke. It is not the refined aesthetic or eloquence of their words that is important here. This art is not for art's sake, but for the sake of the art of living. I am reminded of one patient who in the depths of despair would bring his African drums to my office and drum his dirge. It had a haunting, melancholic beauty, much like Japanese bamboo flute music that blows into your soul like an autumn wind.

LOVING YOUR FATE

Asked once how he had come to terms with his life, Christopher Reeve said, "You play the hand you're dealt. I think the game's worthwhile." To humbly accept your life as it is, with its diminishment and suffering, is to embody not only the mystical idea of happiness, but also the mystical idea of *amor fati*, or *loving your fate*. Embracing your fate, even in the darkest circumstances, is an act of love—love of yourself and your life, love of the world in its fickleness and cruelty, and yes, love of God. *Amor fati* expresses Jesus' teaching, "resist not evil," at its deepest and most spiritual level. A profound avowal of faith when we have lost all reason to have faith, this act of trust, love, and surrender says to God, as again Jesus did, "not my will, but thine, be done." But it makes no difference here whether we believe in God or not. Reeve was a professed atheist, as was Nietzsche, who made the ancient idea of *amor fati* popular in modern times. Regardless of our religious belief, reducing our resistance to the events of the universe puts into motion a harmony with the universe. This harmony is a living spiritual testimony as much as faith in God: we flow with things exactly as they unfold.

The love of fate needs to be contrasted with fatalism, with a belief in a predetermined universe in which all events have been preestablished and there is no free will. The love of fate does not deny the importance of free will and personal responsibility, nor suggest that events cannot or should not be humanly shaped. "Fate" as it is understood here describes events that constitute the way the universe is unfolding, and to love fate is to willingly follow these events wherever they take us, changing them for better when we can, and bowing to them when we cannot.

As Jungian analyst James Hollis writes, when we willingly embrace our fate, we transform whatever elements in it *seem* fatalistic or like a cruel act of the gods into material for our individuation or personal growth. At that moment, we are no longer *forced* into our fate, but *choose* it. From this we may discover, perhaps some distance down the road, the unique blessings this fate may have in store for us, if not the blessings we had hoped for ourselves at the outset of our life journey. As Joseph Campbell said, "We must be willing to get rid of the life we planned, so as to have the life that is waiting for us." The fate that awaits us is usually more difficult than the one we have planned, but once we choose to accept it, our resistance no longer magnifies the difficulty. We make peace with our fate.

When Reeve said, "I think the game's worthwhile," what could he have known about his fate that we on the outside cannot imagine? The existential psychologist Viktor Frankl, reflecting on his own fateful experience in Auschwitz, believed that courageously taking up our cross adds dignity and a deeper meaning to our lives. It reveals to us whether we are, as Dostoevsky would say, worthy of our suffering. Discovering this makes the game worthwhile. This is beautifully illustrated in Sophocles' tale of Oedipus, who, haunted by his tragic fate until he was finally able to make peace with it, found redemption.

Jung also explored this question of living up to our fate after he suffered a near-fatal heart attack that thrust him into the grips of a severe depression. Here he additionally wrestles with the self-blame we often have when we feel responsible for our difficult fate:

> Something else, too, came to me from my illness. I might formulate it as an affirmation of things as they are: an unconditional "yes" to that which is, without subjective protests—acceptance of the conditions of existence as I see them and understand them, acceptance of my own nature, as I happen to be. At the beginning of the illness I had the feeling that there was something wrong with my attitude, and that I was to some extent responsible for the mishap. But when one follows the path of individuation, when one lives one's own life, one must take mistakes into the bargain; life would not be complete without them. . . .

It was only after the illness that I understood how important it is to affirm one's own destiny. In this way we forge an ego that does not break down when incomprehensible things happen; an ego that endures, that endures the truth, and that is capable of coping with the world and with fate. Then, to experience defeat is also to experience victory. Nothing is disturbed—neither inwardly nor outwardly, for one's own continuity has withstood the current of life and of time. But that can come to pass only when one does not meddle inquisitively with the workings of fate.

Again we see that although the course of life may diminish us, it is through this diminishment that we may grow. Fate is what happens to us. Affirming our fate is what we choose to do with it. This means accepting not only the events that happen to us, but the personal flaws and mistakes that may have caused them in the first place. For example, if our overambitiousness gets us into trouble, then this character trait needs to be accepted as a part of our fate as much as the trouble that consequently comes to us. As Jung said, we must accept our own nature and ourselves as we happen to be, for this too is part of life. This is not to give us a free pass to keep reenacting our flaws and mistakes, but rather to consciously acknowledge them in order to be whole and to learn from them so that we don't impulsively reenact them. As long as we are willing to struggle with our dark aspects, we are not condemned to be a victim of them. This is why *amor fati* is not fatalism or doom, for free will—the capacity to respond to life in new ways—also remains a part of our basic human nature.

Our character is thus often discovered, tested, stretched, and refined through diminishment. The superfluous is peeled off, painfully, and what remains and endures is who we really are. Since our calling to a particular vocation or mission in life is foreshadowed in our character, it, too, is often discovered and forged through some ordeal of diminishment. Perhaps no figure in recent history demonstrated this better than Churchill. Reminiscing on his election as prime minister, he said, "I felt as if I were walking with destiny, and that all my past life had been but a preparation for this hour and for this trial." But Churchill knew better than anyone that his fate was intertwined with the suffering he had endured—his depression, numerous political setbacks, and the death of one of his daughters. This diminishment was a fire that steeled his character. Had he not been seasoned this way, who knows if he would have been able to shepherd Britain through its own diminishment and near-vanquishment in World War II?

But not only great figures forge their character and discover their calling and fate by first falling to their knees. Larry, a 28-year-old African American, grew up in the inner city and was a heroin addict by age 20. He had a job as a janitor and supported his habit by engaging in criminal activities. He came to see me to get help. After detoxification in a hospital and beginning a 12-step program, Larry became overwhelmed by the depression he had been anesthetizing for years. In our sessions he revealed that as a teenager he had hopes of becoming a professional basketball player, but these were dashed by his failure to get into college. My focus was to help him tolerate his feelings of grief, dejection, and worthlessness without relapsing into drug use, and also to help him rekindle his hope.

One session Larry came in and told me that after our previous meeting he had run into his high school basketball coach, who invited him to come to his old school and assist him in coaching students on the basketball team. He did this for the next three months, after which time he decided to take a course to improve his qualifications to get into college. He wanted to get his teacher certification and become a high school coach. Eventually he did both, finding a fulfilling vocation and a renewed sense of purpose in life.

Often fate is that which makes you become the most you can be by way of making you become the least that you are. Certainly, it is not easy to accept being the least, but this may be a vital part of what loving your fate is about. Thoreau got it right when he was able to say, even as he was gravely ill and dying at the age of 44, "I love my fate to the core and rind." That kind of experience, of being the most even at your least, tells you that you are truly living your life fully—when even in profound diminishment, you love it to the core and rind.

LIVING A LIFE OF FEW HOPES AND EXPECTATIONS

Many people today, particularly in America, suffer from what can be called a happiness complex. Although this complex is observable everywhere and is an overt characteristic of our culture, it is suffered quietly because its very nature is to deny suffering. Its sole function is to seek happiness. At its core, this complex appears to be rooted in the perennial search for happiness and in the archetypal longing for paradise.

Like a persecution, guilt, or inferiority complex, the happiness complex is fundamentally an illusion. The illusion is not the belief that one is happy when she is not, although some people will go to any lengths to convince themselves and others that they are happy when they are not. The illusion is rather in the beliefs of what happiness is. Many people today assume that happiness implies the absence of suffering and struggle, as if a life of meaning, service to others, or tormented but creative accomplishment is not also a happy life. Another misconception is that happiness must be sought and acquired, as if it were something special that is apart from ordinary, everyday life. It must be attained by fulfilling some requirement—perhaps making more money or finding a new spouse—or by following some prescribed method or program of self-improvement. But happiness is *right before our eyes*, immediately available to us if we surrender to what this very moment offers, to what fate has put on our table right now. The happiness complex consists of the hope that happiness will come *if only* . . .

This hope is not the kind we would want to nurse. It sucks the spirit dry by funneling it into the syndrome most characteristic of the happiness complex, that of chasing the reflection of the moon on the water: the more we hope to find happiness by pursuing it, the more it eludes us. That the American "pursuit of happiness" has become identified with this syndrome is unfortunate and the root of much *un*happiness. In and of itself material happiness *is* attainable by our efforts, but as many have discovered, it does not guarantee spiritual happiness. The latter, in contrast to material happiness, is attained less by what we *do* or what we *have* than by how we *see*. In whatever context we speak of the way of the small or whichever of its principles we are discussing, we are dealing more with how we see things than with the things themselves. The art of happiness, as the Dalai Lama calls it, is an *art of seeing*. Its premise is that happiness is a state of mind, a prosperity of awareness rather than affluence.

In addition to the hopeless illusion of finding happiness by chasing after it as if it were an object, there are other syndromes that come with the happiness complex. Craving what you don't have and not enjoying what you do are two of the more common ones. These, too, are a matter of how we see things, and how we see our fate. *To crave what you don't have is to cast a shadow where there is none; to not enjoy what you have is to not appreciate the light.* Both fail to penetrate what is. All these syndromes are forms of idolatry, of worshiping false gods and ideals, false hopes and expectations. They are false because of the assumption that the things hoped for or expected are necessary for our happiness. Yes, these things—whatever they may be: money, success, marriage, family—may add to our enjoyment of life, but they are not absolute prerequisites for our spiritual happiness. Happiness, again, is a state of mind.

We all hope for good health and love in our lives, and most of us hope that the world our children inherit will be better than the one we live in now. We expect, or at least should expect, basic human rights—the right to work and be a functional member of society, the right to be treated decently, and all the democratic rights. We also expect our friends to be loyal, our children to be respectful, our government to serve us in our best interest, and things like that. Without basic hopes and expectations, we lose our distinct human character and become no different than the rest of the animals in the animal kingdom. But the hopes and expectations of the happiness complex belong to another order. They serve a fantasy system rooted in what Freud called the pleasure principle and what Buddhism understands as the universal desire to escape suffering. Wanting a kind of happiness that is obtained "out there" and that is seen as an antidote to suffering generates hopes and expectations that would not be so harmful if they were *only* illusions. The problem is that they create a reality of their own, but not the one grounded in Freud's reality principle or Buddhism's existential realism. Like the distorting mirrors and sloping floors of a fun house, they create impressions of the real world that are just real enough for us to pursue but are nonetheless false. The hopes and expectations of the happiness complex give a false impression of the meaning and nature of happiness, and in doing so detract from real happiness. As Edinger said, "Happiness equals what we have, divided by what we expect."

In other regards, too, our hopes and expectations can affect us positively or negatively. If we are fighting an illness, hope is essential. Any period of diminishment or darkness is better endured with a healthy hope that our efforts to survive it are not in vain. Expectation in the sense of anticipating something can also be nourishing, for example, expecting a new baby and preparing for its arrival, or waiting for a dream to come and help us with a particular problem. But unrealistic or inflated hopes and expectations fuel diminishment and darkness rather than soothe them. In inciting us to escape from suffering, they only prolong it or give it a personal sting. When our plight doesn't respond to our hopes and expectations, we conclude that we've been somehow cursed or selected for this fate: "Why me?" we ask. But it's not personal. Suffering is just a part of life, a sore fact that the happiness complex prevents us from accepting.

The mystics teach that a good life is *a life of few hopes and expectations.* Not only does this soothe diminishment and darkness, but deepens and advances them. The soothing and the deepening are not opposites, but go together. After all, we cannot deepen our diminishment and darkness if we are "freaking out" from them. The mystics have cultivated disciplines that soothe while they deepen our diminishment. Again, they expressly wish to gravitate *towards* diminishment and the desert, not *away* from them. Embracing diminishment is their key to both God- and self-realization. As the Christian mystic Meister Eckhart said, "To the extent that you eliminate self from your activities, God comes into them—but not more and no less." And: "To get at the core of God at his greatest, one must first get into the core of himself at his least, for no one can know God who has not first known himself." The life of few hopes and expectations helps us to eliminate our self-centeredness and get into the core of ourselves at our least. We come to know ourselves *and* God because we have been razed down to our essence.

In times of darkness, living with a minimum of expectations can actually help us "hang in there": when we don't demand and expect things to become better according to some preconceived notion, we don't break if they don't. On the other hand, if things do become better, we receive them with an open mind that doesn't clutch at them with dependency. The following Taoist story conveys this spirit of equanimity amidst dark happenings:

There was an old farmer who had worked his crops for many years. One day his horse ran away. Upon hearing the news, his neighbors came to visit. "Such bad luck," they said sympathetically.

"We'll see," the farmer replied.

The next morning the horse returned, bringing with it three other wild horses. "How wonderful!" the neighbors exclaimed.

"We'll see," replied the old man.

The following day, his son tried to ride one of the untamed horses, was thrown, and broke his leg. The neighbors again came to offer their sympathy on his misfortune.

"We'll see," answered the farmer.

The day after that, military officials came to the village to draft young men into the army. Seeing that the son's leg was broken, they passed him by. The neighbors congratulated the farmer on how well things had turned out.

"We'll see," said the farmer.

It is not that the farmer had no feelings about his fate (or, for that matter, his son's fate). Rather, he had no expectations about how it would or should turn out.

Finally, the Sufi poet Rumi also expresses this farmer's fluid attitude but with an appreciation of grace and *amor fati*:

> *This being human is a guest house.*
> *Every morning a new arrival.*
> *A joy, a depression, a meanness,*
> *some momentary awareness comes*
> *as an unexpected visitor.*
>
> *Welcome and entertain them all!*
> *Even if they're a crowd of sorrows,*
> *who violently sweep your house*
> *empty of its furniture,*
> *still, treat each guest honorably.*
> *He may be clearing you out*
> *for some new delight.*
>
> *The dark thought, the shame, the malice,*
> *meet them at the door laughing,*
> *and invite them in.*
>
> *Be grateful for whoever comes,*
> *because each has been sent*
> *as a guide from beyond.*

To live a life of few hopes and expectations is the supreme expression of the way of the small.

ANTICIPATING DEATH'S SMALL PORTAL

Most of our discussion has focused on the way of the small as a code of living. But it also has something to say about dying, the final, concluding event of our lives as well as the most diminishing one. As mentioned earlier, death is the absolute minimalist, taking away our very lives and all that we cherish. It takes our bodies; it takes us away from our loved ones and everything we know in life; it even takes us away from our-selves *as we know ourselves* to a condition we know nothing about. Death is a total and ultimate mystery.

Whatever this mystery may be, one thing, however, is certain: the more encumbered we are with desires, attachments, and negative emotions such as fear or hatred, the more difficult will be our passage from life to death. In my work with the dying, I have observed that the greatest obstacle to a peaceful death, more than any physical suffering, is invariably some form of psychological baggage or unfinished business. The film *Jacob's Ladder* powerfully illustrates how our attachments and yearnings prevent us from letting go to death and act as thorns in our side, making the experience of passing a most torturous one. To have a peaceful death, we need to be small. As such, the way of the small helps us to have not only a good life, but a good death.

The principles for living small are an excellent preparation for the process of dying. If we have lived our lives simply and by focusing on essentials, our consciousness will be molded into a form that is small enough to pass through the keyhole of death with ease. The skills learned in embracing the diminishments we have suffered in life will help us embrace the ultimate diminishment we will undergo when we die. For *these* reasons could Thoreau say even while he was dying, "I love my fate to the core and rind." His fate was to live small, and in doing so, he could face his death with resignation, courage, grace, and love. The art of dying, like that of living, is an art of the small. Perhaps it is mostly in this regard that it is said that life is a preparation for death.

But the way of the small prepares us for death in another important regard, too. In making everyday life sacred, it helps us to approach death—a natural and ordinary part of life—as a sacred event. Here, too, Thoreau serves as an exceptional role model. Listen to his description of how he lived his life:

> The art of spending a day! If it is possible that we may be addressed, it behooves us to be attentive. If by watching all day and all night, I may detect some trace of the Ineffable, then will it not be worth the while to watch? Watch and pray without ceasing? . . . . To watch for, describe, all the divine features which I detect in Nature. My profession is to be always on the alert to find God in nature—to know his lurking places.

From here it was not a far leap for Thoreau to conclude that death, too, is one of God's lurking places. "Death," he wrote, "is beautiful when seen to be a law, and not an accident. It is as common as life." He had a simple attitude toward death, his own included. Thoreau scholar Victor Carl Friesen tells us that when Thoreau was dying, "he was asked if he had made his peace with God; his reply was that they had never quarrelled. When someone else asked him about the next world, he said: 'One world at a time.'" Thoreau faced death as he did life.

The portal or passageway to death—the transition from life to whatever is beyond life—is itself small not only in the sense that if we take baggage and unfinished business with us we will have a thorny, torturous experience. It is small also in the sense that it may not give us a lot of time to prepare. The most mysterious, concluding event of our lives may come to us as a small moment to be seized. Think of those people on the upper floors of the World Trade Center when the airplanes struck on 9/11. Some had barely a few minutes to decide if they should fall to their deaths or burn to death. Up to this moment their day had been unfolding as any other previous day had. Death announced itself suddenly, and the portal to it, though dramatic and traumatic, was in fact short and small. As Marcel Proust reflected, "We say that the hour of death cannot be forecast, but when we say this we imagine that hour as placed in an obscure and distant future. It never occurs to us that it has any connection with the day already begun or that death could arrive this same afternoon, this afternoon which is so certain and which has every hour filled in advance." The corollary of this is "live every day as if it were your last." This of course does not mean you should not plan for tomorrow, but rather that you should savor today.

Such thoughts may at first strike us as gloomy, but if we accept them as reflections on the natural law of life, as Thoreau did, they may empower us to live fully and to psychologically and spiritually prepare for our deaths. This is not to say that we should dwell upon our deaths, for that would be an insult to life. But we should contemplate our mortality, our *finishing*, so that we may appreciate it as the entryway to the eternity that awaits us (however one may conceive this eternity). Such contemplation makes us more human, not less. The diminishment of death, if the world religions and their mystics are to be believed, is the opening of our humanity to its greater condition. Wouldn't we want to face this momentous event as consciously and as prepared as possible? It is in our best interest that we *anticipate death's small portal* so that when the time comes we can pass through it peacefully, traveling lightly like the passing voyagers that we are.

POTENT QUOTES

To arrive at that which you know not
You must go by a way that you know not.
To arrive at that which you possess not
You must go by a way that you possess not.
To arrive at that which you are not
You must go through that which you are not.

[ST. JOHN OF THE CROSS]

[It is about] failing or betraying some mission you were mandated
to fulfill and being unable to fulfill it and then coming to under-
stand that the real mandate was not to fulfill it but to stand guilt-
less in the predicament in which you found yourself.

[LEONARD COHEN, ON THE INSPIRATION FOR HIS SONG,
"THE TRAITOR"]

I want to learn how to walk down the ladder gracefully. I have this
image—I'd like to get smaller and smaller in a relevant way.

[CARLY SIMON, REFLECTING UPON HER MASTECTOMY
AND OTHER PERSONAL LOSSES]

CHAPTER SEVEN

PRACTICING THE WAY OF THE SMALL IN THE WORLD

I do not know wherein I could be better than the worm. For see: he does the will of his Maker and destroys nothing.

[RABBI MENAHEM MENDEL OF VITEBSK]

Today we are faced with the preeminent fact that, if civilization is to survive, we must cultivate the science of human relationships—the ability of all people, of all kinds, to live together and work together, in the same world, at peace.

[FRANKLIN D. ROOSEVELT]

A SLICE OF SMALLNESS

Jungian analyst Clarissa Pinkola Estés tells the following story about her work with survivors of the Columbine High School tragedy. This episode shows the way of the small not only in the world, but also at its best.

> There was a man at Columbine who was a janitor there at the time. When you met him, you might not relate to him right away because he often said one or two things in a sort of nervous mantra, "Hi, Hi, Howya doin?

Howya doin? Good? Good? OK! OK!" Others at the school told me they sometimes wanted to say to him, "Alright, enough already. We already said hello, and how are you, twice now at least."

Some of the students seemed to not like this little janitor. They seemed annoyed by him. I was told some would make fun and imitate him. Students told how some other students would turn the janitor's rolling trash barrel over, spilling all the refuse he had collected so humbly. He was in many ways a very patient man. I once saw him pick up his overturned barrel, set it back upright, pat it all back together again, and say to those who had overturned it, "Hi! Hi! Howya doin? Howya doin?"

In the cafeteria surveillance films, the silent video of the day of the shootings, you see fire and smoke. You see students, some of whom are truly rooted to the spot like deer in the headlights. You see that they have been startled and cannot immediately grasp what is occurring. They cannot think where, what to do next. We cannot hear them, but shots are being fired. Then, you see suddenly, this huge milling of students. It looks like a whirlpool made of human beings. Some are still wearing their backpacks. Some are wearing baggy trousers. Some are wearing white baseball caps. Later the students will tell me you can see at the edge, this figure, blurred, coming in, that this figure is yelling at the stunned students to "Get down!" In the next few minutes, this figure begins grabbing shocked students and throwing them out of the picture.

The students will report later that this blurred figure, this person running back and forth so fast, who began grabbing students by the seats of their pants, by their shirts, their arms, their shoulders, and just throwing them out the door, that this blur of muscle, certainty and eternity, was the little janitor.

The students tell me that this janitor was somehow able to grasp what was going on immediately. While many students were still wondering if this was a stage play by the theatrical department, or a spoof from the computer video class, the janitor was able to throw students toward the doors that were not locked. He was yelling, "Run! Run for your lives! Run!" Many lives were saved that day by a fellow who usually just likes to say "Hi! Hi! Howya doin? Howya doin?"

After the conflagration in the cafeteria, then, with his big skeleton key set, the same keys that some of the kids used to hide from him to trick him, with those in hand, he, in the midst of all the smoke and all the horror, went up and down all the halls, up and down stairwells, completely unguarded with his little chest wide open, locking all the doors of the classrooms, sequestering away many of the terrorized students into classrooms so the shooters could not easily enter and attack them.

Then, because he was a janitor and knew his way around the school, he did something else. . . . You may have heard that it took many hours before the police and SWAT teams entered the building. It is true, and during those horrible long hours, many students and teachers were in anguish hiding inside.

The little janitor could have fled the school, but he did not. Instead, he removed some ceiling tiles and started crawling through the ceilings of the school. A group of students and teachers had rushed into a tiny closet and were standing butt to belly, hour after hour, with the fire alarms going, with the smoke and water, and not knowing whether they would live or die. A student told me that all of a sudden, in that closet, the frightened group huddled there saw fingers coming through the seams of the ceiling overhead. They were terrified. One of the ceiling tiles lifted up. It was the little janitor: "Hi! Hi! Howya doin! Howya doin!"

HUMILITY IS THE HIGHEST FORM OF GREATNESS

According to the Greek historian Herodotus, the wealthy King Croesus asked the sage Solon whether he had ever met a happier man. Solon replied that humble people were often happier than the wealthiest kings. Of course, this was not the answer Croesus was hoping for: it did not validate his belief that he who is wealthy and rules over other men also rules in happiness. This common belief still prevails today. Especially in America, Tocqueville writes, everyone has been liberated from the old aristocratic order to become a king in his own right, so the pursuit of wealth and privilege has become a natural prerogative, the first above all others. In an age when, as a popular rock band sings, *everybody* wants to rule the world, it is refreshing to find a person who is content to be exactly who he or she is, with or without wealth and privilege.

This in fact is the real meaning of the classical, Christian, and Franklinian virtue of humility. It is not about imitating a preestablished ideal of modesty or lowliness, for example, aspiring to be like Gandhi. It would be immodest for a person who is not cut out to be a saint like Gandhi to force his temperament and personality into some mold of what he thinks he should be. Rather, humility is about living graciously within your own natural "mold," according to your own natural capacities and limits. As the Rev. C. H. Spurgeon said, "Humility is to make a right estimate of one's self." To be humble means to know who you are and to be happy with who you are. Humility is very closely related to *amor fati*, but as the attitude that makes *amor fati* possible, it is a subject in its own right.

It is noteworthy that the word "humble" comes from the Latin *humilis*, which means low, small, or slight, and is related to *humus*, the soil or earth. Being humble is that principle of the way of the small that shapes how we see ourselves in our relationship to the world. This principle has always been associated with the earth: the humble person, as far as his own prestige and the admiration from others are concerned, keeps a low profile, and hence is close to the earth. In Confucian thinking, the earth itself is seen as modest: though far greater than we are, it is below us and is what our feet walk on. Similarly, when Jesus said, "Blessed are the meek, for they shall inherit the earth," he meant that the earth and all its fruits belong to the humble. And the opening quotation above by the Hasidic Rabbi Mena-hem Mendel exalts the worm, creature of the earth. Another rabbi, when asked why people no longer see the face of God as they were once able to, answered, because nobody is willing to stoop so low. William Wordsworth concurred: "Wisdom is ofttimes nearer when we stoop than when we soar."

In the social realm, this principle has profound implica-tions. In ancient times, to be of humble origins and lowly was universally seen—Croesus and the ruling classes notwithstand-ing—as the opposite of degradation or a status of "less than," *for the earth sustains all living beings*, a role that only God can also claim. In the early feminine mystery religions, the "Great Earth Mother" was herself a goddess worshipped for her role as a great provider sustaining life (though she also represented the underworld). The peasant farmer who works the land has al-ways been a model of humility and service to his fellow man. The significance of the baby Moses being drawn from the reeds of the Nile and similar ancient redeemer stories did not escape the understanding of the people who lived by them. The divine may have resided up in the heights of Mt. Sinai or Mt. Olympus, but for the most part, the human encounter with it occurred down below. To be small and lowly meant to embody and bring the divine into the human world. The chief servant and messenger of Jesus, who almost single-handedly brought Christianity to the pagan world, may have changed his name from Saul to Paul not only to mark his conversion and fit in better in the Roman world, but also because the Latin *paulus* means "the small," "the humble."

To be humble also meant, in the ancient world, to serve. And to rule like the earth, or like Moses or St. Paul, meant that one served others humbly. How different this was from the ideal prevalent through much of history since those times, including not only the long period of European monarchies but even modern democratic times. To be a king today, whether as a corporate CEO or an NBA star or a movie star is quite literally to be that: a star, something high and lofty, but not necessarily of much earthy service to the people below. Of course, there are a number of stars who support public or other worthy causes, such as Bono who has campaigned for Third World debt relief or Robert Redford who established the Sundance Institute and Film Festival to promote small, independent films. Both these causes advocate the way of the small. But they are exceptions. Even our politicians, supposedly elected to serve, often seem more preoccupied with their own self-interest. The plethora of public scandals in America attest to this, not to mention the know-it-all haughtiness and mud-slinging of our political campaigns. Our modern kings and queens may aspire toward greatness, and some of them may even attain it in some form or another, *but are they small?* How can they be if we don't expect them to be, if we ourselves don't live by this principle?

* * *

Possibly the greatest act of humility is forgiveness. To let go of our bitterness when others have hurt us requires us to be very small, and very strong. We must here rule over ourselves, in particular, our hunger for revenge. Forgiveness is a state of redemption that *we* need to earn, rather than the other who in fact may be incapable of asking for forgiveness. And it is a gift we give to ourselves as much as to the other, for it frees us from the tyranny of our bitterness, anger, and hatred. Yet forgiveness cannot be prematurely forced, otherwise it is false. People who have, for example, been abused by loved ones must never leap over their anguish and anger in an act of pseudoforgiveness. Genuine forgiveness must be patiently prepared for by working through our feelings of victimization. This can be painstaking. Nor should forgiveness be a way to avoid confronting others when necessary. It is not a way to dismiss or get around their wrongful behavior; this may need to be addressed directly. All the same, forgiveness does not depend merely on their expiation or apologies. It happens in *our* hearts. It sees the transgressions of others not with the passion of revenge, but with compassion toward their fallen humanity—which we all share in common—even if this fallen humanity is something *they* cannot see. This Godlike ability to see the transgressions of others with compassion is what Alexander Pope was referring to when he famously said, "To err is human, to forgive, divine."

Earlier I mentioned how Abraham Lincoln embodied the small even in victory by encouraging a humble and forgiving attitude toward the South. This was an exquisite example of forgiveness in collective life, of practicing the way of the small in the world at large. Another remarkable example of this in modern times is the unprecedented transformation that took place in South Africa, the transfer of power from whites to blacks and to majority rule. Who would have thought that this transfer could have happened so peacefully? This was one of the great miracles of the twentieth century. One would have imagined that after generations of racial domination, exploitation, and cruelty, blacks would have vented their rage violently. Only leaders with spirits like Nelson Mandela and Frederik W. de Klerk could have spearheaded this transformation without mass hysteria and bloodshed. The new government's Truth and Reconciliation Commission, with its impassioned but civilized hearings, was a collective demonstration of humility, forgiveness, and the way of the small unlike any other in history. It opened the door to healing. The political philosopher Hannah Arendt was right: "Forgiveness is the key to action and freedom."

APPROACHING DIVERSITY AND COMPLEXITY BY WAY OF THE SMALL

The way of the small requires us to relate to the diversity and complexity of the world. Tolerating people's differences and understanding their complexity are necessary in modern times. Even the way of the small itself is diverse and complex, showing us many faces. It is expressed not only in the world's religions, but in science, too. Subatomic physics, molecular and cell biology, molecular genetics, chaos theory and fractal geometry, and nanoscience are all unique windows on the way of the small. Each offers a special view of the world. Clearly, there are *many* ways of the small.

Diversity and complexity demand harmony. The principle that many small things converging together lead to greater things may be observed in many areas of life, the social sphere being the most obvious. A society by definition is a gestalt or whole that is greater than the sum of its many small parts. The way of the small has the important role here of negotiating how these parts come together to create a functional whole that is fit and satisfying for human life. The way of the small, although expressed first and foremost in the smallest unit of humanity—the individual—does not exist in a social vacuum. It can also be expressed creatively through the collaboration of many individuals.

The key factor affecting the way of the small in society is not the numbers of people involved, but their spirit or consciousness. This is the crucial ingredient of the way of the small in any scenario, whether social or not. The smaller the group, the more dynamically will the way of the small likely express itself. As both Freud and Jung believed, the individual's consciousness—meaning his self-reflection, free will, and integrity—descends to its lowest common denominator in large groups. This is the fallibility of mass psychology, of the "group mind," and the reason why large groups and mass movements tend to become immoral or amoral and behave, as Freud said, like a herd of animals. The framers of the U. S. Constitution recognized this as well, designing the checks-and-balances system of the American government partly to counteract this tendency. However, there are examples of large bodies of people who have more or less consciously expressed the way of the small in their culture and history, most notably, the ancient Chinese, the Jews, the Native Americans, and other tribal peoples. We may here add the Tibetans as another example of a people who embody the way of the small—not only in their culture and religion, but in the humble, patient way they have endured their diaspora while their leaders have struggled to make their cause known on the world stage.

In the life of organizations, institutions, our economy, and the international political theater, the way of the small can make the difference between failure and success, high and poor performance quality, stability and instability, inflation and recession, war and peace. One may think of the collapse of the dot.com companies and the bullish stock market in the late 1990s, and Alan Greenspan's term "irrational exuberance" to describe the inflated mindset that led to it. George W. Bush's invasion of Iraq without an adequate plan for the occupation of it offers a chilling illustration of the destruction, turmoil, and loss of life that can result from ignoring diversity and complexity (in regard to both Iraqi society and the details of reconstruction). The way of the small encourages us to be clearly aware of diversity and complexity—if not always have control over them—so our actions don't come back to bite us. Unfortunately, such clarity, together with the sound judgment it goes hand-in-hand with, is in dire shortage in our troubled global village. More than ever, it is needed.

This raises an intriguing notion: if greatness lies in being small, then a great nation, no less than an individual, should aim to be small. Being small, as can be gathered from everything discussed thus far, is less about size than, again, one's spirit or consciousness. It is a principle, an ethic, an attitude. A nation the size of America could conceivably practice the way of the small if it made this its intention and applied itself. Less is more, simpler is better, being ordinary but exceptional, celebrating the right details, being small-and-smart, being situated in the world in a strong but humble way, ruling through service, operating by the power of love in contrast to the love of power—what might these principles lead to if applied in a collective context, on a national and global scale? Their implications for health care, education, race relations, environmental protection, urban renewal, economic development, and almost every area of civic life are many. A superb example of the way of the small in a collective context is Muhammad Yunus, the "banker to the poor." A Bangladeshi economist and Nobel laureate, Yunus set up a "microcredit" banking system that "micro-lends" small amounts of money to poor people in Bangladesh and 130 other developing countries. Millions have been empowered to establish small businesses, lifting themselves out of poverty by their own initiative and ingenuity.

Although being small has less to do with size than with one's spirit or attitude, it is inaccurate to say that size is an insignificant issue, especially in the global context. We would not wish to spiritualize the way of the small in such a fashion as to have no bearing upon the actual, material world we live in. It is an accepted fact of history that larger collectives are not guaranteed a longer life span than smaller ones, and given their unwieldiness, they may even reach their peaks and decline sooner. The specific reasons for this, of course, are complex and vary. The Roman Empire lasted 450 years; the Mongolian Empire, the second largest in history, lasted 200 years; the British Empire, upon whose expanse the sun never set, was history's largest, yet it saw its final sunset 350 years after establishing its first settlement in North America. The Byzantine Empire and the Holy Roman Empire were among the few to last over 1000 years, though the latter never functioned as a single nation-state but rather as a religious confederation the way the European Union today is an economic confederation. In short, the way of the great has yet to prove that it can outlive the way of the small, or that the quality of life it provides is greater than that of the way of the small. Thus did Lao-tzu, himself an archivist for the imperial court of China, write, "Let there be a small country with few people."

The way of the small is especially important for the ecology of our planet. We must learn to live more modestly if we wish to conserve energy, reduce pollution, preserve our tropical rainforests and oceans, ensure the survival of endangered species, and eliminate the human contribution to climate change. While there is still much debate about how many people the Earth can support, there can be no doubt that it is a finite number, and that our rapidly increasing population places a heavy burden not only on the environment, but also on the societies that must feed and otherwise sustain that population. The economist Leopold Kohr, who supposedly coined the phrase "Small is beautiful," writes: "If a society grows beyond its optimum size, its problems must eventually outrun the growth of those human faculties which are necessary for dealing with them." In *Small Is Beautiful: Economics As If People Mattered*, Kohr's colleague, E. F. Schumacher, pinpoints some of the factors responsible for the dangerous situation facing the world today:

> General evidence of material progress would suggest that the *modern* private enterprise system is—or has been—the most perfect instrument for the pursuit of personal enrichment. The *modern* private enterprise system ingeniously employs the human urges of greed and envy as its motive power, but manages to overcome the most blatant deficiencies of *laissez-faire* by means of Keynesian economic management, a bit of redistributive taxation, and the "countervailing power" of the trade unions.
>
> Can such a system conceivably deal with the problems we are now having to face? The answer is self-evident: greed and envy demand continuous and limitless economic growth of a material kind, without proper regard for conservation, and this type of growth cannot possibly fit into a finite environment. We must therefore study the essential nature of the private enterprise system and the possibilities of evolving an alternative system which might fit the new situation.

In the final analysis, the way of the small may be the required diet for a small planet, a planet with so many people and competing interests. Before the world can advance toward a more harmonious condition, we must *approach its diversity and complexity by way of the small.* Of course, the place to begin is at home, in our own families, organizations, ethnic groups, and nations. We must begin small.

THE WORLD SCORNS THE SMALL

In 1981, I left a comfortable job as a young college professor and embarked on a career in mental health. During the course of this I held a couple of administrative and leadership positions. These were nowhere near as shielded from the school of hard knocks as the ivory tower of the college (although academic politics could be every bit as harsh as politics anywhere else). Looking back, I could say that almost every mistake I ever made in those positions, whether regarding an organizational issue or an interpersonal one, could have been avoided if I had observed the way of the small. Thinking and acting too big in situations that required an understanding of the small always led to conflict or trouble, or magnified those conflicts and problems that were by nature an unavoidable part of social life. As indicated above, such thinking and acting are also typical of our leaders in government and at the head of our public and financial institutions. This is a universal problem. We all suffer from it. It has often made me wonder: *What is it* about human nature that makes it so inclined toward grandiosity and so repelled by smallness?

One response to this question is that people reject the way of the small because it is a way of the spirit, and the spirit is often experienced as being in opposition to the material world that people so worship. The way of the small, of course, is *not* in opposition to the material world. Indeed, it is discovered *in* the material world and *is* the material world, and thus, if anything, is a *bridge* between the spiritual and material worlds. But the way of the small may be *perceived* as opposed to the material world because it makes the material world small—not insignificant, but small. Or at least it limits the relentless gratification of our appetites in the material world. The importance that being small gives to spirituality and that spirituality gives to being small has been denied by man since he first built the Tower of Babel—a symbol of material gratification, empire building, and grandiosity par excellence.

This spiritual factor is what renders the way of the small sublime and almost ethereal—one reason why legend portrays Tom Thumb and Thumbelina as coming from the realm of the fairies. But this factor is also what renders it so difficult—in some ways, more difficult than the ways of the material world. Spirituality is not only invisible, but is, literally, second nature to us (in comparison to our physical, biological nature which has a much older history of evolution). We naturally resist and have little patience for the demands of spirituality, and in particular, the way of the small. In addition to asking us to stop and take stock of who and what we are, the way of the small asks us to make sacrifices to serve it. This is why Thoreau, in spite of his popularity, is hardly mainstream.

An understanding of why the world rejects the way of the small may also be gleaned from the legend of Lucifer and the fall of creation. Such legends or symbolic stories hint at profound truths, and this one is especially concerned with human nature and the nature of the world. Lucifer was one of God's archangels, among the highest if not *the* highest in the hierarchy of angels. Originally his role was to bring light to the world: the word "Lucifer" means "light-bringer." Not satisfied with his position, he led a rebellion of angels against God. When he was defeated and cast into hell, God did not take away his power. Jesus refers to him as the "prince of this world," implying that when Lucifer fell, he not only brought all of creation down with him but continued as its ruler. His tempting Adam and Eve and their exile from the Garden of Eden—another version of the fall of creation—goes hand-in-hand with this.

But what was the fall of Lucifer about? Legend says that Lucifer fell because of his ambition to replace God as the lord of creation; being an archangel wasn't enough for him. He wanted to step into God's shoes and be God himself. (The Gnostic tradition offers an interesting twist to this: it claims that Lucifer was outraged upon learning of God's plans. Not only did God intend to elevate humankind above Lucifer, a celestial angel, but he also planned to so completely diminish *himself* as to eventually incarnate as a man—a diminishment known in Christian theology as "kenosis." But the motivating factor of Lucifer's behavior is here the same: the sin of pride, or inflation.) Lucifer wanted to be bigger and more important than he was. Lucifer symbolizes not only evil or darkness, but bigness or inflation. The ruling principle of the world then, if we follow this reasoning, is the ambition to be large like God (or what we think is God). Indeed, history, with its constant rise and fall of nations, empires, and civilizations, is very much the story of human ambition and inflation. Most of the evil man has perpetrated has been a consequence of this.

As you make your way in the world, approaching its diversity and complexity by way of the small and striving to be small yourself, remember: *the world scorns the small.* Plainly, its chief operating principle is contrary to it. The way of the small is a small principle in a world of large ambition and inflation.

DEALING WITH YOUR OWN SHADOW

It is disheartening to take stock of the problems that plague our world. It may be preferable to say, "I'm so small, the world is so big, what can I do?" However, that is *not* the way of the small; it is just small-minded, not to mention, irresponsible. If we are to understand how to live the way of the small in the world today, we must understand the *nature* and *meaning* of the darkness in the world and how to work the way of the small in light of this darkness. This is perhaps a curious juxtaposition of imagery, to work in light of darkness, but appropriate.

"The world," Jung said, "hangs by a thin thread, and that thread is the psyche of man." What he meant is that consciousness is the critical ingredient of human salvation. Without it, we are doomed, for our own *unconsciousness* of our dark side and propensity toward evil, combined with the powers we have today to annihilate ourselves, are deadly. The only factor that reduces the danger of this deadly combination is our awareness that *we* are the weapon; the weapons outside us and the causes we use them for are but the triggers. Consequently, as Gandhi said, "We must be the change we wish to see in the world." Again, we come to the vitally important principle of *seeing*. Seeing that the human psyche, with its love of destruction, is itself the greatest danger ushers in not only awareness, but humility, trepidation, and cautiousness—qualities sorely needed in times such as our own. Perceiving others to always be the danger, while not seeing oneself as an equal danger, is also hazardous. This leads to the hot polarization that characterizes so many of the conflicts in the world today. Always the other is evil, but we are righteous. Seeing all this changes the equation, for as the Heisenberg principle states, the act of observing a phenomenon changes it. Jung adds:

> If you imagine someone who is brave enough to withdraw all these projections, then you get an individual who is conscious of a pretty thick shadow. Such a man has saddled himself with new problems and conflicts. He has become a serious problem to himself, as he is now unable to say that *they* do this or that, *they* are wrong, and *they* must be fought against. He lives in the "House of Gathering." Such

a man knows that whatever is wrong in the world is in himself, and if he only learns to deal with his own shadow he has done something real for the world. He has succeeded in shouldering at least an infinitesimal part of the gigantic, unsolved social problems of our day. These problems are mostly so difficult because they are poisoned by mutual projections. How can anyone see straight when he does not even see himself and the darkness he unconsciously carries with him into all his dealings?

This passage voices the spirit of the way of the small. It is a psychological amplification of Jesus' teaching that only when we first cast out the beam in our own eye shall we see clearly to cast out the mote in our brother's eye. Jung here shows the importance of consciously seeing our darkness: the darkness in the world can only be transformed when we face and own it as *ours*. This is primarily an *individual* task, not a collective one. It needs to happen collectively, but must take place in the individual soul—in each person's psyche—as an expression of that person's effort and development. The collective body of humankind can only be as conscious, evolved, and humane as the individual members that comprise it. This is the way of the small: you focus on your piece, I focus on mine. We each do our part "in shouldering at least an infinitesimal part of the gigantic, unsolved social problems of our day." This, of course, is not to say that collective efforts such as social activism and community work are unimportant. *They are crucial.* Rather, it is to say that without the light of personal consciousness to illuminate them, these efforts are bound to fail or at least be lame, for they will never penetrate the real problem.

❊ ❊ ❊

"Man is not the lord of beings. Man is the shepherd of Being. Man loses nothing in this 'less'; rather, he gains in that he attains the truth of Being. He gains the essential poverty of the shepherd, whose dignity consists in being called by Being itself unto the preservation of Being's truth."

The passage you just read, if you contemplate it, trumpets the way of the small in a quiet tone and with a serene wisdom that are well-suited to it. "Man is not the lord of beings." He is small. "Man is the shepherd of Being." He is, in his role of service, privileged. He is "called by Being itself unto the preservation of Being's truth." These words were written by Martin Heidegger, one of the twentieth century's greatest philosophers, and one of the great philosophers of all time. He was also, like many of Germany's intellectuals at the time, a bona fide member of the Nazi party, a curious fact that, in its absurdity and grotesqueness, speaks to the crisis of consciousness in modern times. How could a man who has so eloquently given voice to the most spiritual of the operating principles of the way of the small, insist on being part of the most wicked example of inflation in the history of the world—so much so that, even after the war, he never recanted? Some suggest that the nervous breakdown he suffered in 1946 involved a recognition of his guilt.

It is not my intent to diminish Heidegger or his contribution. I merely raise his example as a matter of profound and dark irony. To advocate the way of the small without correctly applying it to the moral dimension, as appears to have been the case with Heidegger, is a dangerous sleight of hand. When we do this, we feign being the shepherd of Being's truth while really running with the wolves that want to kill it. This is usually a self-deception more than a deception of others. We see another variation of this dynamic in collective life everywhere: the boss, salesperson, politician, priest, or helping figure who claims, and genuinely believes, to be humbly doing something for the good of others while really harming or taking advantage of them. The way of the small must include moral conscience and be concerned with moral choices. The importance of morality for the good life is why ancient philosophers like Socrates and Cicero and more recent ones like Spinoza and Kant gave such detailed attention to ethics.

To take a stand against evil in the world, in whatever form and context one finds it, is to assert the way of the small in the most human way possible. It is here that our greatest frailties and vulnerabilities, our proneness to be complicit with error or wrongdoing, come into question. Again, as Jung said, to take a stand against evil in the world does not imply only the evil out there in others, but first and foremost in ourselves. The following dream shows the connections between the way of the small, the delicate factor of consciousness, and the moral choice of taking a stand against one's own wrongdoing as well as another's. The dreamer is a high school teacher, and the dream came in response to an incident of reprimanding his disrespectful adolescent son, Tim. The father had enforced his authority in a brusque, authoritarian, schoolmaster-like way, and the son exploded and stormed out of the room, resulting in a period of chilled relations between the two. It was clearly a situation in which they became polarized, yet identical in their opposition to each other: both felt the other was disrespectful and wrong.

> I'm in Tim's 6th grade class in the back of the room. I've snuck in and the teacher doesn't know I'm there. The chairs and tables are too small for me. We have to do a project and I can't decide what the theme of my project should be. The other kids have all chosen a project and are working on it. An inner voice tells me, "Choose sincerity," which I think is strange because it's a social studies class. Shouldn't I choose a social studies topic? The inner voice says, "It's okay, sincerity is what you should choose." So I choose it and think, "How should I do this? Lectures, charts and graphs, pictures, personal presentation?" The idea is, it does not matter as long as I choose "sincerity."

The father recognized that although he was right to reprimand his son for misbehaving, his way of going about it was inappropriate and unhelpful. He acknowledged that in treating his son as if he were one of his unruly students, he alienated him. His association to the small chairs and tables was twofold. On the one hand, he felt the dream was telling him that he was "bigger than that," meaning that he didn't have to get into a power struggle with his son. On the other hand, he felt it was telling him that he was *too* big, that he needed to come down to his son's level. This meant relating to him emotionally, in contrast to the way he had to operate with his students. "With my students," he said, "I don't have the time or luxury to get into their feelings when they're acting out. I have to enforce my authority, and I can't let whether they like me or not get in the way. But it's different with my son. I do care whether he likes me."

This is where the assignment of "sincerity" came in: "I'm a student in the dream because I have something to learn, too," the father said. "I think the dream is telling me I need to be sincere and let Tim know how it makes me feel when he's disrespectful. I need to be vulnerable. When Tim swore at me and stormed out, I was hurt and angry, and then stewed in it for days. That was childish on my part." The dreamer, a patient in therapy, obviously had the capacity to work with his dreams in a creative way. But he also had the maturity to look at his own shadow, not just his son's, and take responsibility for his part. He was willing, as Jung said, to "become a serious problem to himself." Seeing that two wrongs don't make a right, he was able to break the polarized impasse with his son, and their dialogue moved to a new level. Of course, kids being kids, the conflict resurfaced, but the father now had a more authentic and genuinely empowered way of dealing with his son's adolescent rebellion.

I recount this case not because of its parenting merits, but because it illustrates a problem that affects all arenas of human behavior—family, society, and international affairs alike. The problem of splitting off the shadow, projecting it onto others, and polarization is perhaps the chief ailment in the world today (if not always). And as we saw in this father's instructive dream, the only way to deal with this problem, in whatever arena it is encountered, is sincerity. This implies not only honesty—with ourselves as well as others—but genuine receptivity: sitting in the small chair of the other and *seeing* his point of view—not necessarily agreeing with it, but seeing it. I am not suggesting that we ask terrorists how they feel or that we try to relate to them in an emotionally empathic way. Their behavior places them outside the range of that kind of civility. But nevertheless, it is important to understand them in order to comprehend what we are dealing with. And even as we take a stand against their evil, it is important to not lose sight of our own. We must *deal with our own shadows.*

LEARNING TO LISTEN TO SILENCE

Although it is important to work the way of the small in the world as best we can, at the end of the day we must accept that this is not the way of the world. Our smallness must be sustained and regularly rejuvenated by its source—the inner, spiritual world. Also, how the way of the small engages the world must express an interior, spiritual quality, otherwise it would no longer be true to itself. It is not in character with this way to go out and conquer the world like some evangelical movement. How this way moves in the world should reflect the way smallness resonates: quietly. Quietude or silence is golden because it is the language of wisdom, in particular, the wisdom of the small. To listen to silence is to listen to the small. Great and small truths alike are often heard inside our depths when we are silent. They emerge in small moments that can be seized only when we are not distracted by the noise outside us *and* inside us. The wisdom of the small reveals itself to us through that inner voice that needs our silence in order to be heard. As Fred Rogers once remarked, "Real revelation comes through silence."

This makes me think of Elizabeth, a patient who began therapy in a severely depressed, introverted condition. For the first few years she came into my office, sat down, and did not speak a word for forty minutes and sometimes the entire session. She stared out the window, seemingly lost in her inner world. She was not interested in sandplay or drawing, two techniques of nonverbal therapy. At first I tended to interrupt her reverie by asking what she was thinking or feeling. This was sometimes productive but more often was met with the answer, "I don't know." So I learned to just sit with Elizabeth in her silence until she was ready to speak. And then in the last few minutes of the session she would speak softly, and these gems of wisdom about her predicament would crystallize. Gradually over the years her process of self-discovery unfolded out of her pregnant silence. She found her voice in life by going inwards, by seeking out and bringing forth her inner voice, at first heard only faintly. We both had to be small and learn to listen to her silent process.

Silence is the language of wisdom beyond words. As Elie Wiesel said, "There is a certain mystical experience called the purification of language through silence." All mystical traditions extol the virtue of silence, fostering it through meditation and the contemplative life. This is why any discussion of the way of the small sooner or later leads to meditation and contemplation. These forms of focusing the mind are themselves applications of the way of the small, helping us zero in upon the principles of being in the moment and penetrating and flowing with what is. Meditation in particular cultivates a quiet mind and heart, shutting out the vexations of the outer world and creating or revealing a more calm and peaceful inner world. But in truth, this quietness helps us to move in and through the world in a manner that allows the world to be itself, while *we* are in it in a calm and peaceful way. Silence here has little or nothing to do with sound. It is a state of mind. It is what the inside of our mind feels like when it is small. It is not the absence of thought, but the absence of the drivenness or busy-ness of thought. As the Buddhists teach, thoughts always naturally arise. If we don't actively engage them but just watch them, they pass, like clouds moving across the sky. Another analogy is getting into our car downtown. All around us is the noise and clamor of city life. But when we close the door, we drive through the city in silence.

Listen to this story about the smallness and silence of the eighteenth century Japanese Zen master Hakuin Ekaku as he walked amidst the tumult of the world:

Hakuin was praised by his neighbors as one living an exemplary life. One day a beautiful girl in the village was found to be pregnant. Her angry parents demanded to know who the father was. At first resistant to confess, the anxious and embarrassed girl finally pointed to Hakuin. When the outraged parents confronted Hakuin with their daughter's accusation, he simply replied, "Is that so?"

When the child was born, the parents brought it to Hakuin, who now was viewed as a pariah by the whole village. They demanded that he take care of the child since it was his responsibility. "Is that so?" Hakuin said calmly as he accepted the child.

For some months he took very good care of the child, until the girl could no longer stand the lie she had told. She confessed that the real father was a young man in the village whom she had wished to protect. The parents immediately went to Hakuin to see if he would return the child. With profuse apologies they explained what had happened. "Is that so?" Hakuin said as he handed them the child.

This is the equanimity of smallness and silence: "Is that so?" This is not to say that we should passively accept every injustice the world heaps upon us. A quiet mind and heart are not the same as quietism or social indifference, and silence does not mean being mute. This story is a teaching device: again, silence is an inner condition within an outer condition. The outer condition may need to be dealt with on its own terms, but the inner condition remains unperturbed.

As Hakuin well knew, silence draws its strength from the absolute source of life that animates all mysticism. Because the Absolute is ineffable and cannot be conveyed by one person to another, it is best expressed through silence. After years of working on the *Summa Theologica*, a *magnum opus* that attempts to present all of Christian theology as systematically as possible, St. Thomas Aquinas had a profound religious experience. It was so intense that he altogether stopped writing, never finishing his *summa* or summary of theology. In his words, it seemed "like so much straw compared to what I have seen and what has been revealed to me." *That* is the way of the small: we are *reduced* to silence.

POTENT QUOTES

*Forgiveness is the fragrance the violet sheds on the heel
that has crushed it.*

[MARK TWAIN]

*It is no accident that [in alchemy] the gold is to be found not only
"in a heavenly place," but "in stercore," in the dung.*

[ERICH NEUMANN]

*If it be your will
that I speak no more
and my voice be still
as it was before
I will speak no more
I shall abide until
I am spoken for
if it be your will . . . .*

[LEONARD COHEN]

CONCLUSION

*Not that the story need be long, but it will take a long while
to make it short.*

[HENRY DAVID THOREAU]

What a strange paradox: to discover that our deepest joy
lies not in becoming more, but less, not in conquests,
but in surrender, not in acquiring, but in sacrificing. Happiness evades us to the degree that we are not small. Precisely
because it prefers to be small, and we do not, it is often what
we least expect it to be. It is hard to imagine what can come
from surrendering or letting go to the way of the small. And
possibly because of this, it is hard to let go in the first place.
Failure of the imagination and fear of the unknown are perhaps the greatest obstacles to practicing the way of the small.
They even play a part in inflation. We believe we need to com-
pensate our smallness by being godlike and are afraid to discover what being small would do to us. It is true that it would
diminish our self-importance and sense of control over things.
But at the same time, the way of the small would immensely
enrich us.

How would it enrich us? To begin, we would become
smaller in our concentration upon what's important. We

would be keenly involved in the details and circumstances of our lives, yet not defined by the grandiose times and society we live in. We would deal with complexity as best we could, but strive to keep things simple. We would curtail our distractions and egocentric attachments. We would develop a focused way of living, recognizing our limits, our responsibilities, our ordinariness, our exceptional qualities, our capacity to love, our dark side—all the things that make us human. Penetrating our humanity in this way would deepen and broaden it, giving our personhood more weight and substance. Being thus more grounded in ourselves, we would be more fully self-possessed and comfortable in our skin, knowing who we are both in the world and spiritually. Still we would remain humble and try to be of service to others. We would flow with life as it unfolds, but be prepared to go against the grain if necessary. We would take things seriously but with humor. We would try to improve what we can, but accept our fate with equanimity. Surrendering to our smallness would bring inner peace, which in turn would enable us to face our death with composure.

We have seen people in our midst who have lived the way of the small in this fashion: Gandhi, Schweitzer, Mother Teresa, Mandela, to mention just a few. There are many others who are less known or not known at all. Their smallness is what makes them great. What is it that happens to these people to make them change? Few of them were born that way. Many went through a profound diminishment before they became truly small. They underwent a spiritual transformation, a life-altering shift in the way they saw things. But what was it? What is transformed in such diminishment, and what makes it spiritual?

If we allow ourselves to be led by the way of the small to where it wants to take us, eventually we may become so small that we are no longer obstacles to ourselves or the mysterious fate or calling at work in our souls. Diminishment of this kind even leaves behind feelings of loss and the natural panic of losing ourselves. The ego can respond only with silence to something so unfathomable from its point of view. As we become smaller and smaller—emptied and released even from ourselves—we find a spiritual freedom that transcends political, financial, and other kinds of freedom. This freedom is identical to true happiness. It is freedom from our false self—the freedom found in our deep, inner self.

This self is not defined by the world, nor caught up in our egotistic self-importance. It knows that it is only a passing visitor in this fleeting thing called "life," yet intuits its connection to something eternal if not its own eternal nature. It is for this reason that Gandhi, Schweitzer, Mother Teresa, and Mandela all came upon an appreciation of the eternal or divine through the way of the small. And, in their cases, this appreciation was not the esoteric kind characteristic of certain mystics, but an ordinary kind: all found the divine by making everyday life sacred. Mandela even found the divine in a prison cell. But one does not have to be a Gandhi, Schweitzer, Mother Teresa, or Mandela to discover the freedom of the inner self and the sacred in everyday life. They did not reach this discovery through their greatness, but through their smallness—something we also can find within ourselves. And if we do find it, then we, too, can come to our true greatness.

As I conclude this book and reflect upon my own journey into the small, I am drawn to a dream I had when I was four. It is among my earliest memories, and I shall never forget it. At the time I was with my parents vacationing in Lake George, New York. I was very excited about our plans to take a motorboat ride the next day, and all night long I kept waking my father to ask him if it were time to get ready. Each time he told me to relax and go to sleep. Finally I did. And then came the dream. I saw myself go into a small cabin like the one we were staying in that night. When I entered it, I was amazed. Inside was a huge room, much larger than one would expect looking at the exterior of the cabin. There were many wonderful things on display, including toys and tourist trinkets of the kind on sale everywhere in Lake George. Though I naturally could have had no way of understanding this at the time, it was as if the dream were confirming that the small experience of riding a motorboat was an enormous event.

With my understanding today, I can also see that this dream provides an excellent metaphor for the way of the small. The cabin is small on the outside, but large and wondrous inside. This brings to mind G. K. Chesterton's comment, "In everything that matters the inside is much larger than the outside." So it is the same with the way of the small: it is small as far as the ways of the world are concerned, but it is a large and wondrous world in its own right. The way of the small is just like this magical cabin. Given this, I wonder if my childhood dream was more than a childhood dream, and more than a metaphor. Perhaps it was actually portraying that I would one day embark upon the way of the small just like I entered that cabin that night.

We are each at any given moment facing the doorway of our own magical cabin, if not already in it. This cabin is not somewhere else. It stands before us right here, right now. If we listen closely, we can hear a still, small voice deep inside. Its stillness invites us in, and its smallness lets us know that we have arrived home.

NOTES

INTRODUCTION

p. *xvii* Marcus Aurelius, *Meditations*, 7:67. This particular translation is based on John Bartlett, *Familiar Quotations*, 10th edition, Little, Brown and Co., Boston, 1919.

PART ONE: WHAT IS THE WAY OF THE SMALL?

p. 1 Hasidic tale: "The Firmaments," in *Tales of the Hasidim: Late Masters*, ed. Martin Buber, Schocken Books, New York, 1948, 1974, p. 273.

p. 1 Winston Churchill, in Jon Meacham, *Franklin and Winston: An Intimate Portrait of an Epic Friendship*, Random House, New York, 2003, p. 191. Originally in *The Jewish Chronicle*, November 1941.

CHAPTER TWO: WE ARE THE WAY OF THE SMALL

p. 7 Hasidic tale: "Nothing at All," in *Tales of the Hasidim: Early Masters*, ed. Martin Buber, Schocken Books, New York, 1947, 1975, pp. 198–99.

pp. 11–14 *Powers of Ten: A Film Dealing With the Relative Size of Things in the Universe and the Effect of Adding Another Zero*, made by the Office of Charles and Ray Eames for IBM, copyright 1989 Lucia Eames. This film is available on DVD and videotape from the Eames Office, 2665 Main Street, Santa Monica, CA 90405, tel. (310) 396-5991.

p. 16 Niels Bohr, cited in Gary Taubes, "Einstein's Dream," *Discover: The Newsmagazine of Science*, Time, Inc., New York, December 1983, p. 53.

p. 18   Steven Weinberg, *The First Three Minutes: A Modern View of the Origin of the Universe*, Basic Books, HarperCollins Publishers, New York, 1977, 1993, pp. 154–55.

p. 18   Stephen Hawking, in *Der Spiegel*, October 17, 1988.

p. 18   Max Ehrmann, "Desiderata," 1927, 1954.

CHAPTER THREE: GOD'S SMALL SECRET

p. 23   Charles Darwin, *The Origin of Species*, Chapter Four, 1859.

p. 24   Shunryu Suzuki, *Zen Mind, Beginner's Mind*, Weatherhill, New York and Tokyo, 1970, 1979.

pp. 24–25   God's instructions on the design of the ark: Exodus 25:10–22.

p. 25   "Who is wealthy? . . . ," Talmud, *Pirke Abot*, chapter 4:1.

p. 26   "The kingdom of God is within you," Luke 17:21, King James Version.

p. 26   "Whoever becomes small shall understand the kingdom," Gospel of Thomas 3:46.

pp. 26–27   "The kingdom of heaven is like a grain of mustard seed . . . ," Matthew 13:31–32, Revised Standard Version.

p. 27   "Except ye be converted . . . ," Matthew 18:3, King James Version.

p. 27   "[I]t is easier for a camel . . . ," Matthew 19:24, Revised Standard Version.

p. 27   Citation of Jesus on birds and lilies of the field, Matthew 6:25–34, Revised Standard Version.

p. 27   "Render to Caesar . . . ," Mark 12:17, King James Version.

p. 27   "He who is least among you all is the one who is great," Luke 9:48, Revised Standard Version.

p. 28   "My God, my God, why hast thou forsaken me?," Matthew 27:46, King James Version.

p. 28   Koran 2:115, translated with notes by N.J. Dawood, Penguin

Books, Harmondsworth, England, 1956, 1974, p. 344.

pp. 29–30   "The Great Tao flows everywhere . . . ," *Tao Te Ching*, v. 34, in "The Natural Way of Lao Tzu," in *A Source Book in Chinese Philosophy*, translated and compiled by Wing-tsit Chan, Princeton University Press, Princeton, NJ, 1963, 1972, p. 157.

p. 30   Etymology of "yin" and "yang": see Stephen Karcher, *How to Use the I Ching: A Guide to Working with the Oracle of Change*, Element, HarperCollins, London, 1997, p. 6.

p. 30   ". . . let people hold on to these . . . ," ibid., v. 19, p. 149.

pp. 30–31   Confucius on love: passage cited in Huston Smith, *The Religions of Man*, Harper & Row, New York, 1958, p. 174.

p. 31   "Small is the cooing dove . . . ," *Book of Poetry* (also called *Book of Odes* or *Book of Songs*), in James Legge, translator, *The Sacred Books of China: The Texts of Confucianism*, Part I, *Sacred Books of the East*, Vol. 3, Clarendon Press, Oxford, 1879, p. 352.

p. 32   *The I Ching or Book of Changes*, the Richard Wilhelm translation rendered into English by Cary F. Baynes, Foreword by C. G. Jung, Princeton University Press, Bollingen Series XIX, 1950, 1976, pp. 40–43, 239–44.

pp. 33–34   *The Principal Upanisads*, edited with introduction, text, translation, and notes by S. Radhakrishnan, George Allen & Unwin, London, Humanities Press, New York, 1953, 1974, pp. 617, 634–35, 637.

p. 36   Sekito Kisen, "Soan No Gin," or "Strawroof Hut," based on a translation by Étienne Zeisler that is copyrighted by the American Zen Association.

p. 37   C. G. Jung, letter to Walter Robert Corti, April 30, 1929, in *C.G. Jung Letters*, Vol. 1, 1906-1950, selected and edited by Gerhard Adler in collaboration with Aniela Jaffé, translations from the German by R.F.C. Hull, Bollingen Series XCV:1, Princeton University Press, Princeton, NJ, 1973, pp. 65-66.

p. 37   Emily Dickinson, "How happy is the little stone," in *The Poems of Emily Dickinson*, Thomas H. Johnson, ed., Belknap Press of Harvard University Press, Cambridge, MA, 1951, 1955, 1979, 1983.

p. 37   William Blake, "Auguries of Innocence," first published in 1863, probably written 1800–1803; in *The Complete Poetry and Prose of William Blake*, edited by David V. Erdman, University of California Press, Berkeley, 1982, p. 490.

PART TWO: ESSENTIAL PRINCIPLES FOR LIVING SMALL

p. 39   Lao-tzu, *Tao Te Ching*, v. 48, op. cit., 1963, 1972, p. 162.

p. 39   Rainer Maria Rilke, "The Man Watching," in *Selected Poems of Rainer Maria Rilke: A Translation from the German and Commentary by Robert Bly*, HarperCollins, New York, 1981, pp. 105, 107.

CHAPTER FOUR: BUILDING A FOUNDATION

p. 41   "In reading the lives of great men . . . ," Harry S. Truman, handwritten memorandum dated May 14, 1934, in the Longhand Notes File, President's Secretary's Files, Harry S. Truman Papers. Also appears in *Strictly Personal and Confidential: The Letters Harry Truman Never Mailed*, edited by Monte Poen, Little, Brown and Co., Boston, 1982, p. 138.

p. 41   "The goal is to make the ego as strong and as small as possible," C.G. Jung: this was personally communicated to James Kirsch who in turn related it to Charles Zeltzer.

pp. 41–43   *Chicago Tribune* cartoon and caption cited in David McCullough, *Truman*, Touchstone/Simon & Schuster, New York, 1992, p. 482; quotations from Truman, pp. 402, 726, 384, 459; references to his life as a public servant, pp. 231, 233, 272, 392–93, 437–40; reference to Marshall Plan, p. 564; quotation from Dean Acheson, p. 755; and assessment by McCullough, p. 991.

p. 44   Joni Mitchell, concert with Bob Dylan and Van Morrison, Pauley Pavilion, UCLA, Los Angeles, May 1998.

p. 45   Gilda Frantz, "Being Ageless: The Very Soul of Beauty," in *Psychological Perspectives*, Vol. 50, Issue 1, 2007, Routledge: Taylor & Francis Group, Philadelphia, PA.

p. 45   "Simplicity, simplicity, simplicity!" Henry David Thoreau, *Walden*, Barnes & Noble Books, New York, 1993, p. 75.

pp. 45–46   "I went to the woods . . . ," Henry David Thoreau, ibid., p. 75.

p. 53   James Hillman, *Suicide and the Soul*, Harper & Row, New York, 1964, p. 73.

p. 54   "If there is a worse place . . . ," Abraham Lincoln, in Michael Burlingame, *The Inner World of Abraham Lincoln*, University of Illinois Press, Urbana, Chicago, 1994, p. 105.

p. 56   "We must be careful . . . ," *The I Ching or Book of Changes*, op. cit., p. 130.

p. 56   Confucius, *Analects*, cited in Huston Smith, op.cit., p. 165.

p. 57   "All beginnings are small," C. G. Jung, in *C.G. Jung: Psychological Reflections*, op. cit., p. 310.

p. 57   Lao-tzu, *Tao Te Ching*, v. 64, popular translation rendering Chinese measurements into miles.

p. 57   Dante Alighieri, *The Divine Comedy*, "Paradiso," Canto 1, line 34.

p. 57   "Difficulty at the beginning works supreme success," and commentary, *The I Ching or Book of Changes*, op. cit., pp.16, 17.

pp. 57–58   Lance Armstrong, *It's Not About the Bike: My Journey Back to Life*, Berkley, New York, 2000, 2001, pp. 50–51.

p. 60   Marie-Louise von Franz, *The Feminine in Fairy Tales*, Spring Publications, Zurich, 1972, 1974, p. 58.

p. 61   "My religion consists of . . . ," Albert Einstein, in Lincoln Barnett, *The Universe and Dr. Einstein*, with a Foreword by Albert Einstein, Bantam Books, New York, 1948, 1974, p. 109.

p. 62   "[T]he superior man of devoted character . . . ," *The I Ching or Book of Changes*, op. cit., p. 179.

p. 63   Sun Tzu, *The Art of War*, translated and with an introduction by Samuel B. Griffith, Foreword by B. H. Liddell Hart, Oxford University Press, 1963, 1984.

p. 63   "Everything is ready . . . ," Winston Churchill, in "Churchill," PBS, October 15, 2003.

p. 64   "Be ye wise as a serpent, and gentle as a dove," Matthew 10:16.

p. 66   Malcolm Gladwell, *The Turning Point: How Little Things Can Make a Big Difference*, Back Bay Books/Little, Brown and Co., New York, 2000, 2002, pp. 142–46.

p. 69   Bob Dylan, in *Bob Dylan: In His Own Words*, edited by Christian Williams, Omnibus Press, Book Sales, London, New York, 1993, p. 32; quotation dated 1987.

p. 69   "Everything should be made . . . ," attributed to Albert Einstein, cited in *Reader's Digest*, October 1977.

CHAPTER FIVE: FINDING HAPPINESS

p. 71   Samuel Johnson, *The Rambler*, section 6, April 7, 1750, in *The Works of Samuel Johnson*, Vol. I, Electronic Text Center, University of Virginia Library.

pp. 71–72   "The Voice of Happiness," in *Zen Flesh, Zen Bones: A Collection of Zen and Pre-Zen Writings*, compiled by Paul Reps, Anchor Books, Doubleday, Garden City, NY, p. 30.

p. 72   Alan Watts, *The Meaning of Happiness: The Quest for Freedom of the Spirit in Modern Psychology and the Wisdom of the East*, Perennial Library, Harper & Row, New York, 1940, 1970, p. 102.

p. 76   Friedrich Nietzsche, *Twilight of the Idols, or How to Philosophize with a Hammer*, "Maxims and Arrows," aphorism 12.

p. 79   George Harrison, "All Things Must Pass," *All Things Must Pass*, Harrisongs Music, Apple Records, New York, 1970.

p. 81   T. S. Eliot, "Burnt Norton" (1936), Quartet No. 1 in *Four Quartets*, 1943.

pp. 82–83   On the canalization of libido: see C.G. Jung, *Symbols of Transformation: An Analysis of the Prelude to a Case of Schizophrenia*, Vol. 5 of *The Collected Works of C. G. Jung*, translated by R. F. C. Hull, Bollingen Series XX, Princeton University Press, 1956, 1967.

p. 84   Tennessee Williams, *A Streetcar Named Desire*, University of the South, 1947, New American Library, New York, 1951.

pp. 84–85   Lance Armstrong, op.cit, pp. 67-68.

pp. 85–86   Jack Riemer, "Itzhak Perlman Improvises," *Houston Chronicle*, February 10, 2001. It is to be noted that there is no evidence that Perlman performed at Lincoln Center on November 18, 1995, the night Riemer claims this episode took place, and his account has come under scrutiny. Nevertheless, more important than its historical veracity is the truth of its message.

p. 90   Donald Kalsched, *The Inner World of Trauma: Archetypal Defenses of the Personal Spirit*, Routledge, London, New York, 1996.

p. 91   Edward F. Edinger, *Ego and Archetype*, Penguin Books, Baltimore, MD, 1972, 1973, p. 153.

p. 92   On God's sense of failure and disappointment with his creation of man: see Genesis 6: 6–7.

p. 94   St. Paul, 1 Corinthians 13: 4, 5, Revised Standard Version.

pp. 94–95   Passages on feeling: James Hillman, in Marie-Louise von Franz and James Hillman, *Jung's Typology*, Spring Publications, Dallas, TX, 1971, pp. 135–136, 169.

p. 96   Hermann Hesse, "How Heavy the Days" (1911), in *Poems*, selected and translated by James Wright, Farrar, Straus and Giroux, New York, 1970, p. 43.

p. 101   Citation from Holocaust survivor: Chaya Ostrower, "Humor as a Defense Mechanism in the Holocaust," doctoral dissertation at the University of Tel Aviv.

p. 101   Murray Horowitz, "A Conversation on American Comedy and the Catskills Legacy," a symposium at New York University, April 2002.

p. 103   Leonard Cohen, "Anthem," *The Future*, © Leonard Cohen Stranger Music (BMI), Sony Music Entertainment/Columbia Records, 1992.

p. 103   Mother Teresa, cited in Gayle Heiss, *Finding the Way Home: A Compassionate Approach to Illness*, QED Press, Fort Bragg, CA, 1997, p. 63.

CHAPTER SIX: EMBRACING DIMINISHMENT

p. 105   "When you think that you've lost everything . . . ," Bob Dylan, "Tryin' to Get to Heaven," *Time Out of Mind*, © Sony Music Entertainment/Columbia Records, 1997.

p. 105   "The experience of the self . . . ," C.G. Jung, *Mysterium Coniunctionis: An Inquiry into the Separation and Synthesis of Psychic Opposites in Alchemy* (1955–56), Vol. 14 of *The Collected Works of C.G. Jung*, translated by R.F.C. Hull, Bollingen Series XX, Princeton University Press, 1963, 1970, p. 546. Italics are Jung's.

pp. 105–107   Artist's account: taken from Clark E. Moustakas, *Loneliness*, Prentice-Hall, Englewood Cliffs, New Jersey, 1961, p. 52.

p. 108   St. John of the Cross, *The Ascent of Mount Carmel* and *The Dark Night*, in *The Collected Works of St. John of the Cross*, translated by Kieran Kavanaugh and Otilio Rodriguez, with Introductions by Kieran Kavanaugh, ICS Publications, Institute of Carmelite Studies, Washington, D.C., 1973.

p. 108   Dante Alighieri, *The Divine Comedy*, "Inferno," Canto 1, lines 1–3.

p. 108   Leo Tolstoy, *A Confession, The Gospel in Brief, and What I Believe*, translated and with an Introduction by Aylmer Maude, Oxford University Press, London, 1961.

p. 110   On the cyclic process of psychological growth: Edward F. Edinger, *Ego and Archetype*, op. cit., pp. 41–42.

p. 111   "It is in this darkness . . . ," Thomas Merton, *New Seeds of Contemplation*, New Directions, New York, 1961, 1972, p. 258.

p. 114   Rainer Maria Rilke, "The Man Watching," op. cit.

p. 114   Clark E. Moustakas, op. cit., pp. 102–103.

p. 115   "Do not look for rest . . . ," Thomas Merton, op. cit., p. 259.

p. 117   "Resist not evil," Matthew 5:39, King James Version.

p. 117   "Not my will, but thine, be done," Luke 22:42, King James Version.

p. 118   James Hollis, *Creating a Life: Finding Your Individual Path*, Inner City Books, Toronto, 2001, p. 66.

p. 118   Joseph Campbell, cited in John D. Goldhammer, *Radical Dreaming: Use Dreams to Change Your Life*, Citadel Press, New York, 2003, p. 66.

p. 119   Viktor E. Frankl, *Man's Search for Meaning*, Pocket Books, New York, 1959, 1976, pp. 106–107.

pp. 119–120   "Something else, too, came to me from my illness . . . ," C. G. Jung, *Memories, Dreams, Reflections,* recorded and edited by Aniela Jaffé, translated by Richard and Clara Winston, Vintage Books, Random House, New York, 1965, p. 297.

p. 121   I felt as if I were walking . . . ," Winston Churchill, in "Churchill," PBS, October 15, 2003.

p. 122   "I love my fate to the core and rind," Henry David Thoreau, in Robert Louis Stevenson, "Henry David Thoreau: His Character and Opinions – Part 1," *Cornhill Magazine*, June 1880.

p. 124   The Dalai Lama and Howard C. Cutler, *The Art of Happiness: A Handbook for Living*, Riverhead Books, Penguin Group, New York, 1998.

p. 125   "Happiness equals . . . ," Edward F. Edinger, *Ego and Archetype*, op. cit., p. 61.

p. 126   "To the extent that you eliminate . . . ," Meister Eckhart, in *Meister Eckhart*, translated by Raymond B. Blakney, Harper & Row, New York, 1941, p. 6.

p. 126   "To get at the core. . . ," Meister Eckhart, op. cit., p. 246.

p. 128   Jelaluddin Balkhi Rumi, "The Guest House," in *The Illuminated Rumi*, translated by Coleman Barks, Broadway Books, New York, 1997.

p. 130   "The art of spending a day! . . . ," Henry David Thoreau, *Journal*, September 7, 1851.

pp. 130–131   "Death is beautiful when seen . . . ," Henry David Thoreau, letter to Ralph Waldo Emerson, March 11, 1842.

p. 131   Victor Carl Friesen, " Seeing Beyond the Verge of Sight: Thoreau's Nature as Incessant Miracle," presented at the Symposium on Science, Spirituality, and the Environment at Brock University, St. Catharines, Ontario, January 21–23, 1999.

p. 131   Marcel Proust, "The Guermantes Way," in *Remembrance of Things Past*, Vol. 6, Part 2, Chapter 1, 1921.

p. 133   "To arrive at that . . . ," St. John of the Cross, *The Ascent of Mount Carmel*, Book I, Chapter 13, verse 11; translation my own.

p. 133   Leonard Cohen, in the film *Leonard Cohen: I'm Your Man*, directed by Lian Lunson, Lions Gate Entertainment, 2005.

p. 133   Carly Simon, in Sara Davidson, "The First Day of the Rest of My Life," in *Newsweek*, January 22, 2007, p. 58; this article is adapted from *Leap! What Will We Do With the Rest of Our Lives?* Random House, New York, 2007.

CHAPTER SEVEN: PRACTICING THE WAY OF THE SMALL
IN THE WORLD

p. 135   Rabbi Menahem Mendel of Vitebsk, in "The Worm," *Tales of the Hasidim: Early Masters*, ed. Martin Buber, Schocken Books, New York, 1947, 1975, p. 177.

p. 135 Franklin D. Roosevelt, final speech (1945), written but never delivered due to his death, in Seth Goddard, "Franklin D. Roosevelt: Leader of the Free World," Hero of the Week Profile, *Life*, April 14, 1997.

pp. 135–138 Clarissa Pinkola Estés, "Explaining Evil," in *Terror, Violence and the Impulse to Destroy: Perspectives from Analytical Psychology* (Papers from the 2002 North American Conference of Jungian Analysts and Candidates), edited by John Beebe, Daimon Verlag, Einsedeln, Switzerland, 2003, pp. 75–77.

p. 139 C.H. Spurgeon, *Gleanings Among the Sheaves*, Baker Book House, Grand Rapids, Michigan, 1977, p. 27.

p. 140 "Blessed are the meek . . . ," Matthew 5:5, King James Version.

p. 140 William Wordsworth, *The Excursion*, Book III, 1814.

p. 142 Alexander Pope, *An Essay on Criticism*, 1711, line 525.

p. 146 Muhammad Yunus with Alan Jolis, *Banker to the Poor: Micro-Lending and the Battle Against World Poverty*, Public Affairs, New York, 1999.

p. 147 Lao-tzu, *Tao Te Ching*, v. 80, in *A Source Book in Chinese Philosophy*, op. cit., p. 175.

p. 148 Leopold Kohr, *The Breakdown of Nations*, Chelsea Green Publishing, White River Junction, Vermont, 1957, 2001, p. 21.

p. 148 E.F. Schumacher, *Small Is Beautiful: Economics As If People Mattered*, Harper & Row, New York, 1973, 1989, p. 280.

p. 151 Jesus on Lucifer: John 12:31, 14:30.

p. 152 "The world hangs on a . . . ," C.G. Jung, "The Houston Films" (1957), in *C. G. Jung Speaking: Interviews and Encounters*, edited by William McGuire and R.F.C. Hull, Bollingen Series XCVII, Princeton University Press, 1977, p. 303.

pp. 153–154 "If you imagine someone . . . ," C.G. Jung, "Psychology and Religion" (1937), in *Psychology and Religion: West and East*, Vol. 11 of *The Collected Works of C. G. Jung*, op. cit., p. 83.

p. 154 Jesus on casting out the beam in our eye: Matthew 7:3–5.

p. 155 Martin Heidegger, "Letter on Humanism (1946)," in *Pathmarks*, edited by William McNeill, Cambridge University Press, Cambridge, UK, 1998.

p. 160 Fred Rogers, "The Charlie Rose Show," KCET (PBS), May 13, 1997.

p. 161 Elie Wiesel, "Facing Hate," a conversation with Bill Moyers, KCET (PBS), 1991.

p. 164 Erich Neumann, *Depth Psychology and a New Ethic*, translated by Eugene Rolfe, Forewords by C.G. Jung, Gerhard Adler, and James Yandell, Shambhala, Boston, 1969, 1990, pp. 145–46.

p. 164 Leonard Cohen, "If It Be Your Will," *Various Positions*, © Leonard Cohen Stranger Music (BMI), Sony Music Entertainment/Columbia Records, 1984.

CONCLUSION

p. 165 Henry David Thoreau, in Robert Louis Stevenson, op. cit.

p. 167 Nelson Mandela, on religion and his experience in prison: see John Battersby, Special to *The Christian Science Monitor*, February 10, 2000.

p. 168 G. K. Chesterton, *The Autobiography of G. K. Chesterton* (1936), Chapter 2, "The Man with the Golden Key," Ignatius Press, San Francisco, 2006.

ACKNOWLEDGMENTS

I have been blessed with family and friends who helped make this book a project of sharing and collaboration. George Gellert carefully read an early draft and made many valuable suggestions. I am also thankful for his love and brotherhood. Charles Zeltzer, a spiritual brother and also a reader, contributed most generously with his time, insight, and small-and-smart wisdom. Also very beneficial were the thoughtful comments of Deborah Wesley, an old friend and a shrewd reader.

Donald Weiser, publisher, has my deepest gratitude for giving the book a home. Valerie Cooper, former editor-in-chief at Nicolas-Hays, enthusiastically shepherded it to the early stages of publication. Yvonne Paglia, current editor-in-chief, masterfully guided it to completion. Kathryn Sky-Peck was everything an editor and production manager could be, applying her creative talents in matters large and small. Kimberley Cameron championed the book and was a great support. Aryeh Maidenbaum, Director of the New York Center for Jungian Studies and also a wise old friend, graciously created a place for it in the Jung on the Hudson Book Series. Robin Palmer gave the manuscript a good close shave.

Jill Danzig of Danzig Communications was indispensable in the launch of this book, and Michael Kerber, Bonni Hamilton, and Amy Grzybinski of Red Wheel/Weiser were immensely helpful in bringing it to a wider public.

Robert Moradi, John Beebe, Jane Murphy, Jennifer Hunter, and Rabbi Gabriel Elias pointed me to material that has been included in the book. Judith Hecker shared her own experience as a psychotherapist working the way of the small. Sensei Nicolee Jikyo McMahon, a most colorful Zen master with a wonderful teaching style, provided a learning environment to explore the Buddhist God of small things.

For their good cheer and more I thank my loving sister-in-law Noelle Gellert, Jerry Barclay, Katharyn Morgan, Arlene TePaske Landau, Bradley TePaske, Eliane George, Agi Orsi, Jeff Goodman, Norman and Harriet Weinstein, Liat Cohen, Brahm and Carole Canzer, Rose-Emily Rothenberg, Daniel and Grace Rothstein, David Deneau, Martha Assima, Jon Straub, Joel Cowgill, Warner and Celia Carr, Annie Chen, Paula Smith-Marder, Gloria Averich, and Voneelya Simmons.

And last but not least, I feel special gratitude to my patients. Much of what I have learned about the way of the small has been from working with them.

ABOUT THE AUTHOR

Michael Gellert is a Jungian analyst practicing in Los Angeles and Pasadena, California. He was formerly Director of Training at the C. G. Jung Institute of Los Angeles and a humanities professor at Vanier College, Montreal. He also supervised a mental health program for employees of the City of New York and has served as a consultant to various organizations, including *Time* magazine. He has lived in Japan, where he trained with a Zen master. The author of *Modern Mysticism* and *The Fate of America*, he lectures widely on psychology, religion, and contemporary culture. For more information, visit www.michaelgellert.com.